ALDOUS HUXLEY

Literature and Life: British Writers

Selected list of titles:

Complete list of titles in the series available from the publisher on request.

ALDOUS HUXLEY

Guinevera A. Nance

A Frederick Ungar Book
CONTINUUM · NEW YORK

1988

The Continuum Publishing Company
370 Lexington Avenue
New York, NY 10017

Printed in the United States of America

Library of Congress Cataloging-in-Publication Data

Nance, Guinevera A.
　Aldous Huxley / Guinevera A. Nance.
　　p.　cm. — (Literature and life series)
　Bibliography: p.
　Includes index.
　ISBN 0-8044-2639-2
　1. Huxley, Aldous, 1894–1963—Criticism and interpretation.
I. Title.　II. Series.
PR6015.U9Z78　1988　　　　　　　　　　　87-29017
823'.912—dc19　　　　　　　　　　　　　　CIP

For Daphne:

> God delights
> In such a being; for her common thoughts
> Are piety, her life is gratitude.
>
> —*The Prelude*

Contents

Chronology

1894   Born July 26 at Laleham, Godalming, Surrey.

1908   Enters Eton, planning to specialize in biology. Julia Huxley dies of cancer.

1911   Suffers attack of *keratitis punctata*, which causes near blindness and necessitates withdrawal from Eton.

1913   Enters Balliol College, Oxford.

1914   Suicide of brother Trevenen.

1915   Visits Garsington and meets Philip and Lady Ottoline Morrell. First meeting with D. H. Lawrence.

1916   Receives a First in English Literature from Oxford. Publishes *The Burning Wheel*. Moves to Garsington.

1917   Accepts teaching post at Eton. Publishes *Jonah*.

1918   Publishes *The Defeat of Youth*.

1919   Joins the editorial staff of the *Athenaeum*. Marries Maria Nys at Bellum, Belgium, on July 10.

1920   Publishes *Limbo*. Matthew Huxley is born. Becomes drama critic for the *Westminster Gazette*. Publishes *Leda*. Begins working for Condé Nast on *House and Garden*.

1921   Publishes *Crome Yellow*.

1922   Publishes *Mortal Coils*.

1923   Publishes *On the Margin*. Moves to Italy. Publishes *Antic Hay*.

1924   Publishes *Little Mexican* and *The Discovery*.

1925   Publishes *Those Barren Leaves* and *Along the Road*. Begins round-the-world journey to India, the Straits Settlements, Java, Hong Kong, and the United States.

1926   Visits the United States. Publishes *Two or Three Graces*. Publishes *Jesting Pilate*. Meets D. H. Lawrence in Florence. Publishes *Essays New and Old*.

1927   Publishes *Proper Studies*.

1928   Publishes *Point Counter Point*, which is selected by the Literary Guild in the United States. Moves to France.

1929   Publishes *Arabia Infelix* and *Do What You Will*. First meeting with Gerald Heard.

1930   Publishes *Brief Candles*. Visits D. H. Lawrence at Vence, France and is with him at his death on March 2. Publishes *Vulgarity in Literature*.

1931   Publishes *The World of Light*, which is produced in London at the Royalty Theatre. Publishes *The Cicadas* and *Music at Night*.

1932   Publishes *Brave New World*. Publishes *The Letters of D. H. Lawrence*. Publishes *Texts and Pretexts*.

1933   Publishes *Retrospect*. Leonard Huxley dies.

1934   Publishes *Beyond the Mexique Bay*.

1935   Becomes active in the pacifist movement.

1936   Publishes peace pamphlet *What Are You Going to Do about It?* Publishes *Eyeless in Gaza*. Publishes *The Olive Tree*.

1937   Leaves Europe and travels to the United States; goes on lecture tour with Gerald Heard. Publishes *An Encyclopaedia of Pacifism*. Publishes *Ends and Means*.

1938   Settles in California. Contracts to write a film script for Metro-Goldwyn-Mayer on the life of Madame Curie.

1939   Publishes *After Many a Summer Dies the Swan*.
        Works on the film script of *Pride and Prejudice*
        for Metro-Goldwyn-Mayer (until January 1940).
1941   Works on the film script of *Jane Eyre* for Twenti-
        eth Century-Fox (until April 1942). Publishes
        Grey Eminence.
1942   Publishes *The Art of Seeing*.
1944   Publishes *Time Must Have a Stop*.
1945   Publishes *The Perennial Philosophy*. Works with
        Walt Disney on a film of *Alice in Wonderland*.
1946   Publishes *Science, Liberty and Peace*.
1947   *The World of Aldous Huxley* is published.
1948   Publishes *Mortal Coils* (stage version of *The
        Gioconda Smile*). The film version of *The
        Gioconda Smile* is released under the title *A
        Woman's Vengeance* (Universal Studios). *The
        Gioconda Smile* opens at the New Theatre in
        London. Publishes *Ape and Essence*.
1949   Paris stage production of *The Gioconda Smile*
        (*Le Sourire de la Gioconde*) opens.
1950   Publishes *Themes and Variations. The Giocon-
        da Smile* opens on Broadway (runs five weeks).
1952   Publishes *The Devils of Loudun*.
1953   Takes mescaline under the supervision of Dr.
        Humphry Osmond.
1954   Publishes *The Doors of Perception*.
1955   Maria Huxley dies on February 12. Publishes *The
        Genius and the Goddess* (the novel).
1956   Publishes *Heaven and Hell*. Marries Laura
        Archera on March 19. Publishes *Adonis and the
        Alphabet* (U.S. title *Tomorrow and Tomorrow
        and Tomorrow*).
1957   *Collected Short Stories* is published. The stage
        production of *The Genius and the Goddess*
        opens on Broadway (closes after five nights).
1958   Publishes *Brave New World Revisited*.

1959   Delivers lectures on "The Human Situation" as
         visiting professor at the University of California
         at Santa Barbara. Receives the Award of Merit for
         the Novel from the American Academy of Arts
         and Letters. Publishes *Collected Essays*.

1960   Becomes visiting professor at the Menninger
         Foundation. Receives radium treatments for
         cancer of the tongue. Takes up Carnegie visiting
         professorship at the Massachusetts Institute of
         Technology and delivers lectures on "What a
         Piece of Work Is Man."

1961   Loses journals, manuscripts, books, and letters
         when house is destroyed by fire.

1962   Becomes visiting professor at the University of
         California, Berkeley. Publishes *Island*. Elected a
         Companion of Literature by the Royal Society of
         Literature. Stage version of *The Genius and the
         Goddess* performed at Oxford and in London.
         Undergoes an operation for the removal of a
         neck gland.

1963   Publishes *Literature and Science*. Writes
         "Shakespeare and Religion." Dies on November
         22 and is cremated. Memorial service held in
         London on December 17.

ALDOUS HUXLEY

1

The Life Theoretic

"An artist is the sort of artist he is, because he happens to possess certain gifts. And he leads the sort of life he does in fact lead, because he is an artist, and an artist with a particular kind of mental endowment."[1] When Aldous Huxley wrote this, he was thinking not so much of himself as of D. H. Lawrence, whose collected letters he was introducing to the public. He was trying to explain why Lawrence's life and art were inseparable and why Lawrence was, in his view, an "artist first of all."

Unlike Lawrence and most of the other writers who came to prominence in the early decades of the twentieth century—James Joyce, Virginia Woolf, T. S. Eliot—Huxley never considered himself to be an artist first of all. He claimed to be the "wrong shape for a story teller" and instead of a born novelist "some other kind of man of letters."[2] His gifts, an extraordinary intellect and a wide-ranging curiosity, disinclined him to restrict himself to any one field of learning or any single literary genre. Over a publishing career that began in 1916 with his first volume of poems and ended with the posthumous publication of an essay on Shakespeare in 1964, he delved into philosophy, political theory, psychology, religion, science, and several other subjects, and wrote in every literary genre. "My primary preoccupation," he wrote a friend, "is the achievement of some kind of overall understanding of the world"; and in poems, plays, short stories, almost a dozen novels, and essays that number into the hundreds, Huxley

1

shares that mental odyssey with his readers. As Francis
Wyndham observed in his 1955 contribution to "A Critical
Symposium on Aldous Huxley," the "fruit of his considera-
ble erudition is lavished on his readers in flattering profusion: quotations from literature, references to art, history
and science—if one takes the allusion, it is with a pleasant
sense of sharing the author's culture, and if not one is
privileged to learn a new fact or to hear an unusual and
provocative point of view."[3]

Aldous Huxley led the sort of life he did in fact lead
because he was among those individuals he once described
as more likely to be philosophers and scientists than poets—those "to whom ideas are as persons—moving and
disquietingly alive." It was the life of involvement with
inquiry and ideas intimated in "The Life Theoretic," a poem published when he was twenty-one. There, he rather
humorously portrays the speaker as having spent his time
"fumbling over books / And thinking about God and the
Devil and all" while others are more actively engaged.
Many years later, in an essay called "Varieties of Intelligence," where he classifies himself as a "moderate ex-
travert" [sic] in intellectual matters, he clearly asserts his
preference for thinking over doing: "I am interested in the
outside world, but only intellectually, not practically. My
ambition and my pleasure are to understand, not to act."

This preeminence of the interior life necessarily renders any attempt to profile Huxley in terms of external
events incomplete. As Alexander Henderson says in his biographical chapter on Huxley, the "excitements are internal, the history psychological. It is a question of describing
a mental development."[4] Yet even though the external happenings of Huxley's life may be secondary, they contain
signposts of the several stages of an internal development
from nihilism to mysticism during which Huxley kept
seeking answers to the question he maintains is fundamen-

tal to philosopher, mystic, and artist alike: "Who am I and what, if anything, can I do about it?"

Aldous Leonard Huxley, whose work best records the answers he made to this question, was born on July 26, 1894, at Laleham, Godalming, in Surrey, into a family with an impressive tradition of intellectual influence. He was the third son of Leonard Huxley and Julia Frances Arnold, who met at Oxford and whose marriage united two of the most distinguished families of the nineteenth century. His father was the son of Thomas Henry Huxley, the brilliant scientist and defender of evolutionary theory who played the role of "Darwin's bulldog" in the mid-Victorian debates over *The Origin of the Species*. His mother was the niece of poet and literary critic Matthew Arnold and the granddaughter of Dr. Thomas Arnold, who as headmaster of Rugby had a far-reaching impact on public-school education in England.

As the offspring of the combined Arnold and Huxley strains, Aldous Huxley possessed a heritage that was at once literary and scientific. And although he is sometimes viewed as having been in his predilections more an Arnold than a Huxley, his legacy from T. H. Huxley is evident in many ways—in his scientific curiosity, in his view of art and science as complementary, in his interest in ethics apart from religious dogma. T. H. Huxley died when his grandson was less than a year old, but Aldous came to know him through his biography and his writings and concluded that he was an "heroic figure of a man."

Although his grandfather was the most prominent figure in Huxley's background, his parents were not without accomplishment. Leonard Huxley was assistant master at Charterhouse when his third son was born. After the success of his two-volume biography, *Life and Letters of Thomas Henry Huxley*, he left schoolmastering to become editor of the *Cornhill Magazine*. In 1901, the family moved two miles from Laleham, to Prior's Field, where Julia Huxley founded and ran a successful school for girls.

Huxley was devoted to his mother, and her death when he was fourteen was the first of several traumatic experiences in his youth that had a lasting impact on him. The second tragedy occurred some three years later, when an attack of *keratitis punctata*, an inflammation of the corneas, caused him to become almost completely blind.[5] His education at Eton, where he had gone in 1908 from Hillside, a preparatory school near Godalming, came abruptly to an end and so did his plans for a career in medicine. Cast largely upon his own resources, he first taught himself to read Braille and then to play the piano, using first one hand to read the score in Braille and playing with the other, and then reversing the process, until he had memorized both parts. As his cousin Gervas Huxley recalls, he faced this disruption of his life stoically and was even able to quip about the benefits of reading Braille. "You know, Gerry," he said, "there's one great advantage in Braille: you can read in bed without getting your hands cold."[6] Although he gradually regained sight enough to "recognize the seventy-foot line" on the Snellen chart at ten feet with the aid of glasses, the infection left his vision permanently impaired.

In the autumn of 1913, Huxley's eyesight was sufficiently improved for him to enter Balliol College at Oxford. That first year was a halcyon time during which he relished the cultural life of Oxford and the companionship of his fellows. Gervas Huxley, who entered Balliol with his cousin, remembers Huxley's being the center of an elite group of students who were drawn to him by the "magnet of his mind, the curiosity of his catholic tastes, and his unassuming friendliness."[7] But this relatively untroubled year was only an interlude. During the late summer of 1914, Huxley's brother, Trevenen, who showed promise of being a brilliant mathematician, committed suicide over an unfortunate love affair.

Still recovering from the loss of his brother, Huxley returned to Oxford to find Balliol practically deserted, his friends gone. World War I had begun, and most of his companions of the previous year had enlisted. Since his defective sight barred him from military service, he experienced the effects of the war primarily through the absence of his friends, many of whom were killed at the front. And this made more acute the memory of other losses—of his mother, and more recently, of his brother. In one of his letters he writes that the war "impresses on [him] more than ever the fact that friendship, love, whatever you like to call it is the only reality." And a few sentences later: "You never knew my mother—I wish you had because she was a very wonderful woman: Trev was most like her. I have just been reading again what she wrote to me just before she died. The last words of her letter were 'Don't be too critical of other people and "love much"'—and I have come to see more and more how wise that advice was. It's a warning against a rather conceited and selfish fault of my own and it's a whole philosophy of life."

It was during the Oxford years, when Huxley had begun to take a serious interest in writing poetry, that a fortuitous meeting with Lady Ottoline Morrell drew him into an elite circle of intellectuals and artists. A patroness of the arts and of young artists, Lady Ottoline made her home at Garsington the gathering place for such guests as D. H. Lawrence, Bertrand Russell, Lytton Strachey, Katherine Mansfield, Middleton Murry, Virginia Woolf, Vanessa Bell, T. S. Eliot, and a variety of others who figure prominently in the beginnings of literary modernism. Garsington was a world apart from the war and from the mores of the post-Victorian age—a society characterized by interesting people, brilliant conversation, and often irreverent views.

Huxley was soon very much at home in this world of the avant-garde, although he was without any literary reputation to speak of at the time. According to Leonard Woolf, he was "immutably himself"[8] among the collection of distinguished guests at a Garsington weekend and was a remarkable conversationalist. Among those who frequented the Morrell home he found friends who shared his interest in the French symbolists and who taught him about modern art. He also found among them the prototypes for several of the characters that were to appear in *Crome Yellow*, his first novel. For more than one reason, then, meeting the extraordinary people who frequented Garsington turned out to be, as Huxley said, of "capital importance"[9] to him.

When Huxley completed his studies at Oxford in 1916, he had a First in English Literature and few prospects for employment. He was anticipating the publication of *The Burning Wheel*, his first volume of poems, in the autumn but wisely recognized that "escaping the workhouse," as he put it, was unlikely if he relied solely on poetry for his livelihood. Two not entirely satisfactory solutions to the problem of a paying profession presented themselves, he wrote to Julian: to "disseminate mendacity on our great Modern Press" or to "disseminate mendacity in our Great Modern Public Schools." Ultimately, he did both. After an eight-month stay at Garsington, during which he worked on the farm, and brief employment as a clerk at the Air Board, he secured a teaching post at Eton. Although teaching was preferable to office work, Huxley was not particularly suited to the life of a schoolmaster. He found the "grim solitudes" of Eton intellectually deadening and the task of correcting essays a distraction from his own writing. Nevertheless, during the Eton period he managed to publish a second book of poetry, *The Defeat of Youth*, the title poem of which draws from the events surrounding the suicide of his brother Trevenen. He also undertook writing a play (eventually reshaped into a short story) because he was convinced that of all the literary genres, plays offered the best moneymaking possibilities; and by that time, he was determined to make writing pay.

Early in 1919, Huxley left teaching and took up what he often deprecatingly called "journalismus." Securing a position on the editorial staff of the *Athenaeum* provided him with the opportunity to fulfill at least partially the desire he had earlier expressed to Julian: "What I want to do is to marry and settle down to write." On July 10, 1919, Huxley married Maria Nys, whom he had met almost four years earlier at Garsington and from whom he had been separated after she returned to her home in Belgium. They settled in Hampstead, and Huxley took on all sorts of assignments to support his family, which soon included a son, Matthew, born on April 19, 1920. In addition to working for Middleton Murry at the *Athenaeum*, he became the drama critic for the *Westminster Gazette*. For a few months, he also worked part-time at the Chelsea Book Club. Finally, he left the *Athenaeum* for a more lucrative position with Condé Nast on the staff of *House and Garden*, where he earned enough to spend a summer in Italy on a brief reprieve from journalism.

Although Huxley returned to England to resume work for Condé Nast, the summer of 1921 in Italy was the turning point in his attempt to establish a literary career. Able, at last, to devote himself entirely to his own writing, he completed *Crome Yellow* in two months. The novel immediately conferred upon him a literary reputation beyond anything occasioned by the publication of his five volumes of poems. And it earned royalties, selling 2,500 copies in the first year. By 1923, its publishers, Chatto & Windus, had offered him the first of what was to become a series of three-year contracts. The agreement called for Huxley to provide two works of fiction per year for three years, one of which was to be a full-length novel, in return for an advance on royalties of five hundred pounds per year.[10] It meant exchanging one kind of writing deadline for another, but Huxley was finally able to see an end to journalism—at least of the sort that restricted him to London and to prescribed topics. "After April," he wrote his sister-in-law in February, "I shall be able to write what I want." He was also able to write where he wanted, and in 1923 he left England for Italy.

This move marked the beginning of Huxley's residence in Europe, primarily in Italy and France, which lasted until 1937. During this period, he traveled extensively throughout the Continent in his four-seater Citroen and took extended journeys to India, the United States, and Central America. Since many of his trips provided him with material for books (*Along the Road, Jesting Pilate, Beyond the Mexique Bay*), they were, in a sense, working expeditions; and, like the legendary *Encyclopaedia Britannica* Huxley is reputed to have carried with him on his travels, they were also a means of satisfying his insatiable appetite for information on an unlimited variety of subjects. He says in an essay that he considers "one of the greatest charms of travel" to consist in the "fact that it offers unique opportunities for indulging in the luxury of ignorance," but his was a short-lived ignorance. Whether scrutinizing a Renaissance painting from the distance of a few inches with the aid of a magnifying glass, or confronting the hills of Jaipur from the back of an elephant, he was apparently always assimilating what he saw and subjecting it to that mental process Kenneth Clark praises as his "power of speedy cross-classification."[11]

After touring India and the United States in 1925, Huxley decided to return to Italy to live and work. In a wry commentary upon his decision, he wrote one of his friends: "Italy seems to me clearly indicated. And after all it's in the grand poetic tradition. Every good English poet, with the exception of Shakespeare, has been to Italy for a more or less lengthy period. It is an indispensable phase in the poetic life." During this phase, Huxley formed a close association with D. H. Lawrence, another in the long line of literary Englishmen who found inspiration in Italy. They had met briefly at Garsington years earlier, and Lawrence had invited Huxley to participate in his scheme to found a utopian colony in Florida. Their reunion and subsequent friendship proved significant for them both—although no two men could have been more different in personality and philosophy. Huxley, the essential aristocratic high-brow, detached and reflective, believed in the power of the intellect; Lawrence, the coal miner's son from Nottingham, sensitive and ebullient, believed in the mystery of the flesh. They differed over the relevance of science and over the nature of knowledge, and they were often critical of one another's work. Huxley felt that too much insistence on the "life business" in Lawrence's novels made them "oppressively *visceral*" and said that in reading them he longed for the "open air of intellectual abstraction and pure spirituality." Lawrence was generally put off by Huxley's novels as well, but admitted to admiring a "sort of desperate courage of repulsion and repudiation in them."[12]

Yet each respected the other despite such fundamental differences. It was Huxley and his wife who were with Lawrence in his last hours and who accompanied Frieda Lawrence to her husband's burial in a remote cemetery in Vence, France. It was also Huxley who collected Lawrence's letters and published them after his death. In his introduction to the letters, Huxley hits upon the basis of a relationship that was built essentially upon contraries: "To be with him was to find oneself transported to one of the frontiers of human consciousness. For an inhabitant of the safe metropolis of thought and feeling it was a most exciting experience."

Given Huxley's inclination to draw fictional portraits in the likeness of people he knew, it is not surprising that Lawrence became the model for a character in *Point Counter Point*, the book Huxley began writing about the time he met Lawrence in Italy and his most successful novel of the 1920s. *Crome Yellow* had launched him as a novelist, and *Antic Hay* and *Those Barren Leaves* had secured for him a reputation as a fictionist and as a portrayer of the postwar generation's cynicism and malaise. But *Point Counter Point*, which best captures the Zeitgeist of the modern age, was a commercial as well as a literary success. It was hailed by the critics and reviewers as a frank and frightening picture of the times and was selected by the Literary Guild in the United States as their book of the month. Although Lawrence found Mark Rampion, the character that resembles him, boring—"a gas-bag"—he was among those who admired Huxley's courage in picturing the wasteland world of the twenties with unflinching veracity. He wrote to Huxley in October 1928, shortly before the novel was published: "I have read *Point Counter Point* with a heart sinking through my boot-soles and a rising admiration. I do think you've shown the truth, perhaps the last truth, about you and your generation, with really fine courage. It seems to me it would take ten times the courage to write *Point Counter Point* than it took to write *Lady C*. [*Lady Chatterley's Lover*]: and if the public knew *what* it was reading, it would throw a hundred stones at you, to one at me."[13]

It was not so much for *Point Counter Point* that the public threw stones at Huxley; it was for his satiric anti-Utopian novel, *Brave New World*. The book was met with hostility and condemnation in many quarters. Numerous public libraries banned it, as did for a time the government of Australia. Huxley's reaction to the Australian ban was that it had certainly given the book an "immense amount of gratuitous advertising." Perhaps because of this advertising, *Brave New World* sold well in England; but it did not initially fare well in either sales or critical reception in the United States. One American reviewer called the novel a "lugubrious and heavy-handed piece of propaganda," and another denounced Huxley for writing "from distaste."[14] Despite this early reception in America, the novel gained in popularity over time and has become, for the average reader, the work most often linked with Huxley's name.

By 1932, when *Brave New World* was published, Huxley's name was synonomous with the philosophical skepticism and intellectual sophistication that characterized 1920s modernism. He was heralded as the spokesman of his age by contemporaries and revered as a liberating influence by the younger generation of readers. According to Stephen Spender, he "seemed to represent the kind of freedom which might be termed *freedom from*: freedom from all sorts of things such as conventional orthodoxies, officious humbug, sexual taboos, respect for establishments."[15] But Huxley was by nature disinclined to settle permanently into any one philosophical mold or to fix on any one novelistic approach. His unfailing interest in the numerous and complex aspects of reality meant that his views evolved and shifted, and so did the intent of his novels. He was, as he says of himself in his essay on Pascal, "a mixed being . . . a colony of free and living minds, not . . . a single mind irrevocably committed, like a fossil fly in amber, to a single system of ideas"; and his music was a "counterpoint, not a single melody."

In 1936, when *Eyeless in Gaza* appeared, it was clear that Huxley's music had changed. Many of those who had relished his work principally for its iconoclasm parted company with him. The new novel reflected his growing interest in mysticism and in proposing solutions for the age rather than merely mocking it from an Olympian height. It also evidenced the influence of Gerald Heard, editor of the short-lived literary magazine, *The Realist*, and writer-cum-philosopher whose answer for psychological and social ills was a personal brand of religious transcendentalism.

Huxley and Heard had met in 1929; in 1935 they were working closely together for the pacifist cause. By this time, Huxley had begun to regard religion as a possible remedy for the world's problems, which were becoming particularly acute under the advancing threat of World War II. He became a sponsor of The Reverand H. R. L. Sheppard's Peace Movement and took to the speaker's platform, from which he proposed that belief in a spiritual reality constituted the best foundation for peace. *Eyeless in Gaza* emerged from the confluence of ideas Huxley had drawn from Heard and from his own growing conviction that the appropriate means to peace were to be found in spiritual awareness. That all of these ideas were gestating at the same time as the novel is clear from one of Huxley's letters, written in November, 1935: "I am working at my book [*Eyeless in Gaza*] and in the interval talking over ways and means, with Gerald, for getting an adequate pacifist movement onto its feet. The thing finally resolves itself into a religious problem—an uncomfortable fact which one must be prepared to face and which I have come during the last year to find easier to face."

In view of his many years of opposition to religion in general and his several published attacks on Christianity in particular, Huxley's discomfort at coming to see religion as a possible antidote for social evils is understandable. Like many of his contemporaries, he emerged from the war years thinking that the world lacked meaning and value— an adherent of the "philosophy of meaninglessness" as in retrospect he called the prevalent doctrine of the early twenties. As late as 1929 he had declared himself to be "officially an agnostic" (just as his grandfather before him had done in coining the word "agnostic" to describe his own position on religion). But by the mid-1930s, he had come to believe that an ultimate spiritual reality informed the world, and he was advocating mysticism as a means of transcending human limitations and of achieving social and spiritual unity. This shift in perspective marked a point of no return in the evolution of his thought and of his writing. Although many of his ideas changed or were modified over the succeeding decades, he never recanted his profession of belief in the mystical experience as a potential avenue for intuiting and uniting with ultimate spiritual reality.

Huxley had begun his philosophical journey toward mysticism in the company of Gerald Heard, and in 1937 the two of them embarked on another voyage that had a lasting impact on Huxley's life. In April of that year Huxley, together with his wife and son, left Europe and sailed with Heard to America for what seems to have been envisioned at the time as a temporary visit but one that ultimately turned into a permanent residency. Inveterate motorists, the Huxleys bought a car in New York and set out across the South and Southwest to explore the country on their way to visit Frieda Lawrence at her ranch near Taos, New Mexico. They stayed in a cabin on the ranch through the summer while Huxley completed *Ends and Means*, which he describes in a letter as a "philosophico-psycho-logico-sociological book on the various means which must be employed if desirable social changes are to be realized." An outgrowth of many of the same concerns and perspectives that produced *Eyeless in Gaza*, this nonfiction book represented Huxley's first attempt to explain systematically his philosophy of non-attachment, an ideal common to both Eastern and Western religions, and to illustrate its efficacy in the social and political realms.

After a few months of traveling about the United States with Heard and lecturing on the theories outlined in *Ends and Means*, Huxley moved to Hollywood to try his hand at writing for the movies. His first assignment was the script for the Metro-Goldwyn-Mayer film on the life of Madame Curie, for which he was paid handsomely and, as it turned out, gratuitously, since his script was superseded when the movie was finally made.[16] Over the years, however, more tangible evidence of his ability to write for a pictorial medium (a kind of writing he found amusing but restrictive) emerged. He produced the film script for *Jane Eyre* and for *Pride and Prejudice* and adapted "The Gioconda Smile," one of his own short stories, for the movies. Issued under the unlikely title of *A Woman's Vengeance* by Universal, the film starred Ann Blyth and Charles Boyer. Shortly after the release of the movie, a stage version of "The Gioconda Smile" opened in New York under the title *Mortal Coils* and in London under the same title as the short story.

Huxley settled in California in 1938, and except for interludes of travel, remained there for twenty-five years. He found friends among the movie greats—Charlie Chaplin, Greta Garbo, Paulette Goddard—and enjoyed a lifelong friendship with Anita Loos, the author of *Gentlemen Prefer Blondes*, to whom he had written a "fan" letter in 1926. He also became acquainted with some of the more influential Hindu teachers in California, most notably Jiddu Krishnamurti and Swami Prabhavananda, who helped him add to his already-considerable knowledge of Indian mysticism. In the early 1940s, he assisted Gerald Heard in establishing Trabuco College, a religious community that Heard led as a sort of resident guru. His continued study of the mystical tradition and of the metaphysical theories underlying the mystical strains inherent in Hinduism, Buddhism, and Christianity had brought him by that time to the conclusion that the intellect was an inadequate tool for understanding ultimate reality; and in his comments at the founding of Trabuco College, Huxley offered a rare glimpse of his own yearning to go beyond the awareness afforded by either intellect or art alone:

I came to this thing in a rather curious way, as a *reductio ad absurdum*. I have mainly lived in the world of intellectual life and art. But the world of knowing-about-things is unsatisfactory. It's no good knowing the taste of strawberries out of a book. The more I think of art I realize that, though artists do establish some contact with spiritual reality, they establish it unconsciously. Beauty is imprisoned, as it were, within the white spaces between the lines of a poem, between the notes of music, in the apertures between groups of sculpture. This function or talent is unconscious. They throw a net and catch something, though the net is trivial. . . . But one wants to go further. One wants to have a conscious taste of these holes between the strings of the net.[17]

The desire to "go further" into awareness, to experience consciously the levels of reality only intimated in art, was one factor in Huxley's readiness to experiment with mind-expanding drugs, mainly mescaline and LSD, in the early fifties. Another factor was his scientific curiosity. He had long been interested in the relationship of mind and matter when, in 1952, he came upon a report of the research that Dr. Humphry Osmond, an English psychiatrist, was conducting with mescaline in exploring the connection between schizophrenia and chemical disorders. He wrote to Osmond, and the two became friends and frequent correspondents. When Osmond visited California, Huxley offered himself eagerly as a "guinea pig," as he puts it, for the doctor's mescaline research—partly because the experiment would allow him to test his notion that mescaline produced effects similar to those of aesthetic and mystical experiences by inhibiting "ordinary brain activity" and "thus permitting the 'other world' to rise into consciousness." Huxley made his first experiment with mescaline the subject of *The Doors of Perception*, a slight but highly controversial book whose title is taken from a line in William Blake's *The Marriage of Heaven and Hell*: "If the doors of perception were cleansed every thing would appear to man as it is, infinite."[18]

In the book, Huxley describes with a certain jauntiness the circumstances under which he took mescaline at this time: "Thus it came about that, one bright May morning, I swallowed four-tenths of a gram of mescalin [sic] dissolved in half a glass of water and sat down to wait for the results." He had hoped the drug would admit him for a time into an inner world of visions; instead it induced him to see the outer world of ordinary objects as sacramental—the furniture, a flower arrangement, even the folds of his trousers, seemed infinite in significance. As he describes it, the episode had overtones of a religious experience, and, indeed, in the book Huxley does equate religion and mescaline in the sense that they are both potential "Doors in the Wall," or means by which people attempt to satisfy their desire for self-transcendence. However, he does not propose that the drug experience is either identical to the mystical experience in the enlightenment it affords or that it should be a substitute for religious insight. Rather, he suggests that the "mescalin [sic] experience is what Catholic theologians call 'a gratuitous grace,' not necessary to salvation but potentially helpful and to be accepted thankfully, if made available."

Over the course of the next ten years, Huxley apparently availed himself of the gratuitous grace afforded by hallucinogens somewhere between nine and twelve times.[19] Since his experiences under the influence of mescaline were so profoundly spiritual, he believed the drug should be taken neither for frivolous enjoyment nor at frequent intervals. The fact, however, that he generally endorsed a chemical route to insight and transcendence in *The Doors of Perception* and in two later books, *Heaven and Hell* and *Island*, created quite a stir. By his detractors and many of his admirers, especially those from what he called the "immense lunatic fringe, eager to tell you about [their] revelation," his work was read simply as propaganda for dope taking. Whether or not it contributed to what became the drug explosion of the sixties is ultimately indeterminable, but it is clear Huxley had no desire to appeal to a wide popular audience that was likely to misconstrue his intentions. In one of his letters to Humphry, he cautions that "we still know very little about the psychodelics [sic], and, until we know a good deal more, I think the matter should be discussed, and the investigations described, in the relative privacy of learned journals, the decent obscurity of moderately highbrow books and articles." Oddly enough, in the last decade of his life, he found himself in a situation similar to one he had described in reference to D. H. Lawrence years earlier—a situation in which his doctrine was invoked by people of whom he "would passionately have disapproved, in defence of a behaviour, which he would have found deplorable or even revolting."

Huxley's closest companion in his explorations into the realms of the psychological and the mystical had always been his wife Maria, whom he affectionately called Coccola. In the winter of 1955, she died of cancer. Huxley's account of her last days, which he recorded shortly after her death and sent to a few friends, describes his use of the lessons from *The Tibetan Book of the Dead* to help Maria die peacefully.[20] In addition to providing a glimpse into an exceptional relationship, this account shows how thoroughly Huxley had woven Eastern thought into the fabric of his life.

The last years of Huxley's life were replete with the satisfactions of a second marriage—to Laura Archera, a longtime friend—and of public recognition. In 1959 he became a visiting professor at the University of California at Santa Barbara, where he lectured on the theme of "The Human Situation," a topic inclusive enough to accommodate his interests in scientific, social, political, and psychological conditions, and which he undertook as an "antidote to academic specialization and fragmentation." That same year, he was given the Award of Merit for the Novel by the American Academy of Arts and Letters, whose previous recipients had included Ernest Hemingway, Thomas Mann, and Theodore Dreiser.[21]

In 1960 Huxley was designated the Centennial Carnegie Visiting Professor at the Massachusetts Institute of Technology and was engaged to present a series of public lectures. He took as his subject "What a Piece of Work Is Man." Two years later, he was elected a Companion of Literature by the Royal Society of Literature. Such academic appointments and literary awards, conferred upon a man who for most of his writing career had chosen not to confine himself to any single problem or province of knowledge, indicate something of the prominence Huxley had gained both within and outside the field of fiction.

From 1960 until his death on November 22, 1963, Huxley lived and worked under the threat of cancer, which first manifested itself as a malignant tumor of the tongue. Radium treatments proved successful, but the cancer later infiltrated the lymph gland of his neck, necessitating the removal of the gland. After the operation, Huxley resumed his pattern of activity, traveling to Sweden to attend a meeting of the World Academy of Arts and Sciences and seeing his last book, *Literature and Science*, through to publication. A relapse confined him to his bed; but, even then, he dictated the final portions of an essay, "Shakespeare and Religion," from his bed and finished it two days before his death.

Huxley thought of himself as an "intellectual with a certain gift for literary art," and in a lifetime devoted to the exploration and presentation of ideas, his enthusiasm for intellectual discovery was unfailing. It was this aspect of his life—the inward journey toward understanding and the full development of his potential as a human being living in a multiplicity of worlds—that came to concern him most. "My life has been uneventful, and I can speak only in terms of being and becoming, not of doing and happening," he said from the vantage point of middle age. Yet in his sixty-nine years, Huxley was a part of a rapidly changing, turbulent era; and it is in his works that he speaks significantly of the "doings and happenings" of man in a complex century.

2

The "Incomplete Man" in the Fiction of the Twenties

In 1926 Edwin Muir, calling Aldous Huxley the "ultra-modern satirist," observed that "no other writer of our time has built up a serious reputation so rapidly and so surely; compared with his rise to acceptance that of Mr. Lawrence or Mr. Eliot has been gradual, almost painful."[1] Muir's comments and Huxley's reputation at the time were predicated principally on three novels, *Crome Yellow, Antic Hay*, and *Those Barren Leaves*, although *Mortal Coils*, a collection of short stories, intervened between the first and the second of these novels. Huxley had yet to publish *Point Counter Point*, which proved to be the culmination of themes and techniques that in the previous novels had occasioned his meteoric rise to fame as the brilliant and bitter spokesman for a disillusioned generation.

Huxley came on the literary scene as a novelist at a time when to be modern meant discarding whatever remnants were left of Victorian values and ideals after science, psychology, and the First World War had taken their toll. Scientific materialism had reduced man to a physiological organism; Freudian psychology had replaced love with the libido; and the war had shattered the ideals of social and political order. With this displacement of traditional values came freedom from all sorts of restrictions—religious, social, artistic—and also despair. For if the sense that everything was "entirely temporary and provisional," as one

Huxley character puts it, made the old taboos seem slightly ridiculous and out of date, it also led to the conclusion that nothing had any ultimate meaning. Huxley describes the prevalent mood of the day in his essay on "Accidie," a concept he defines as the "sense of universal futility, the feelings of boredom and despair." This condition, he suggests, is an inescapable part of the modern consciousness and is for his generation a "state of mind which fate has forced upon us."

In his first four novels, which some of his contemporaries found shocking and others liberating, Huxley both reflected and exemplified the ethos of the twenties. One reviewer of that decade called him "the most perfect representative of the mood he describes."[2] His disillusionment and sophisticated irreverence, echoed by many of the spokesmen for the younger generation in his novels, were in keeping with the age and also helped set a tone for it. Yet despite the fact that these novels were written "by a member of . . . the war-generation for others of his kind," as Huxley said in a letter to his father, they are hardly uncritical portraits of that generation. His depiction of pleasure-seeking young sophisticates making their way in the world according to some notion they have of "living modernly" is charged with satire. He undercuts their self-conscious rejection of traditional values by showing the flimsiness of those they have chosen as replacements; he mocks both their intellectual and their hedonistic evasions of reality. Most pervasively, however, he satirizes the fragmentation that he regards as the chief concomitant of a chaotic age.

Like the inhabitants of T. S. Eliot's Waste Land, who can "connect / Nothing with nothing," most of the characters in Huxley's fictional world lack the ability or the inclination to make connections—either with others or within themselves. They are both socially and psychologically fragmented. On the social level, this lack of connectedness

is illustrated in the novels primarily through noncommunication. Although Huxley's characters talk almost incessant-
ly, conversation being the cornerstone of his technique,
they rarely communicate. The effect can be broadly comic
as characters talk at cross-purposes, or it can be scathingly
satiric, revealing the egocentricity that isolates one character from another. But noncommunication is also more than
a comic or a satiric device. Huxley is substantially rendering his own pessimistic view of social interaction in showing the failure of one individual to establish contact with
another. As Christopher S. Ferns has suggested, Huxley's
consciousness of the "variety of subjective perceptions of
reality"[3] dictated a disbelief in the possibilities of real communication; for if each person has his own private version
of reality, then no common ground of understanding
among individuals is likely. It is this situation of social
isolation that Huxley presents in his fiction and satirizes,
but for which he offers no remedy.

A corollary of Huxley's belief that the multiplicity of
individual perceptions of reality renders communication
impossible is his view that human nature is so "multifarious" (one of his favorite words) as to make psychological
integration a near impossibility for man. "I can make no
order within myself," complains Lypiatt, the grandiose
spokesman for artistic sincerity in *Antic Hay*; and his
plight is one many of Huxley's characters share. Huxley
thinks of man as a divided being, a composite of "mutually
hostile elements," and this concept is fundamental to his
entire vision of man and his predicament. He conveys the
concept in various ways throughout his career and shifts
his views on both the problem and its solution over time;
but the idea that human nature is complex, contradictory,
and conflicted is a preoccupation and a persistent theme in
his work.

Writing in the twenties, at a time when he and his

generation were in what he terms "erotic revolt," Huxley makes the mind/body dichotomy the central illustration of man's divided nature and declares himself heartily opposed to the "excommunication of the body." Thus he directs his sharpest satire in the novels of this period against those who have taken their stand on the side of reason, even though, ironically, these self-conscious intellectuals often tend to resemble Huxley himself. Later, after becoming more mystical in outlook, he emphasizes the complexities of man's tripartite nature, stressing the fact that he is not only "an animal and a rational intellect" but also a "spirit capable of transcendence."

In dealing in his early fiction with the effects of those "diverse laws" of passion and reason that the epigraph to *Point Counter Point* identifies as "self-division's cause," Huxley dramatizes two sorts of problems. One is to be in conflict over the oppositional pull of passion and reason, vacillating between the demands of each; the other is to have essentially dispatched the conflict by denying one of the "laws," or elements of human nature. Huxley sees some danger in the inconsistency of alternating between passion and reason but even more in the consistency achieved through self-denial. Both, however, constitute an imbalance, and from *Crome Yellow* through *Point Counter Point* balance is the fundamental yardstick against which he measures his characters.

The principal object of his satire is the "Incomplete Man," a person who fails to integrate intellect and emotions, to achieve a balance between these contradictions. His ideal, only intimated in the novels before *Point Counter Point*, is the "Complete Man." In an essay called "Spinoza's Worm" in *Do What You Will*, a collection of essays dealing with issues introduced in *Point Counter Point*, Huxley describes this paragon as the "man in whom all the elements of human nature have been developed to the highest pitch compatible with the making and holding of a psychological harmony within the individual and an external social harmony between the individual and his fellows." The Complete Man comes to terms with his divided nature, in Huxley's view, not by denying a part of it but by embracing the contradictions and living fully, with his whole being. Measured by this ideal of the integrated personality, the assorted artists, intellectuals, and hedonists populating Huxley's first novels prove to be an especially fragmented lot and fit subjects for satire.

Crome Yellow

In *Crome Yellow*, Huxley introduces in the protagonist, Denis Stone, a character type that recurs in the succeeding novels of the twenties and those beyond the decade. Denis is a youthful version of the artist-intellectual who retreats from experience and emotion into images and ideas—an early prefiguration of the Incomplete Man. Yet in this novel, such a character is treated more comically than caustically—perhaps because Denis's tendency to intellectualize everything stems partially from his timidity, which he attempts to mask with a façade of erudition and sophistication. He is a Prufrockian sort of character, at once uncertain and egocentric. Like Prufrock, he is "full of high sentence, but a bit obtuse,"[4] and his occasional attempts to act decisively end in failure. However, his foibles and failures, although not entirely mitigated by his youth, are understandable within the context of it. In the opening chapter of the novel, Huxley places the exaggerated self-consciousness and self-importance of this fledgling poet and would-be man of action in perspective with one stroke by commenting that Denis is "twenty-three, and oh! so agonizingly conscious of the fact."

From that point on, Denis is inevitably viewed, for

both good and ill, in light of his youth. His innocence serves as a positive contrast to the hardened cynicism of some of his elders. Yet at the same time, his scholarly pretensions and egocentricity become comically ridiculous against the backdrop of his adolescence. At one point, he diagnoses his problem and admits that "this adolescent business . . . is horribly boring"; but, the narrator adds by way of wry commentary, the "fact that he knew his disease did not help him to cure it."

Denis's eccentricities are the focal point of a book whose purpose is largely to portray people with peculiarities. Conversation through which a character is revealed, rather than plot, constitutes the substance of the novel, which Huxley modeled somewhat after the fiction of the nineteenth-century writer Thomas Love Peacock. Most prominently, *Crome Yellow* has what Huxley calls the "essential Peacockian datum—a houseful of oddities." Assembled for a house party at Crome, the country estate of Henry and Priscilla Wimbush, are a collection of individuals remarkable for their idiosyncrasies and obsessions. For example, the host, Henry Wimbush, is preoccupied with the past and largely uninterested in his contemporary "fellow creatures"; his wife Priscilla is absorbed in astrology and the occult and spends her time casting the horoscopes of racehorses and football players; Mary Bracegirdle, a devotee of Freudian psychology, is solemnly intent on ridding herself of both her repressions and her virginity; Ivor Lombard, a dashing and accomplished Lothario, is devoted to assisting Mary. These characters delight and amuse with their odd behavior, but other characters having more tenuous connections with the Crome society are obviously brought into the novel purely for the sake of ridicule. One of these is Mr. Barbecue-Smith, a kind of secular prophet and writer of spiritual aphorisms, who spends a weekend at Crome preaching the value of "Inspiration." His vapid spiritualism is set in contrast to the stern apocalyptic vision of Mr. Bodiham, the village rector, another adjunct to Crome, who preaches the imminence of Armageddon and waits impatiently for the fulfillment of his doomsday prophecy.

Of all the "oddities" at Crome, two of the most significant from the standpoint of revealing Denis Stone's character are Mr. Scogan and Gombauld, contrasting types personifying reason and passion. Mr. Scogan, whom Huxley describes in reptilian terms, is a sardonic intellectual devoid of either sentiment or sensuousness, a coldly logical man of reason. In contrast, the painter Gombauld, whom Huxley describes as being "altogether and essentially human," is a handsome and passionate Byronic sort dedicated to art and dalliance. Of the two, Gombauld is the more pleasant and Scogan the more penetrating, but neither is a norm in this novel in which all the characters have flaws.

Scogan and Gombauld are each limited by the lack of those characteristics the other possesses. Nature, as Scogan observes, has been "horribly niggardly" in endowing him with passions; Gombauld, a celebrant of teeming life, has no talent for abstraction. But despite their limitations, they each serve to point up Denis's inadequacies as he attempts to play the roles of sophisticated intellectual and passionate poet. Compared to Mr. Scogan's encyclopedic knowledge, the "twenty tons of ratiocination" of which Denis boasts are lightweight learning indeed. At the same time, compared to Gombauld's vital ardor, Denis's passion is sickly romantic yearning. Too cerebral to become directly engaged in life and too sensitive to be a completely dispassionate intellectual, Denis is essentially an escapist from both reason and passion—a retiring idealist who substitutes phrases for feeling and prefers the sound of words to their meaning.

The central irony of the novel is that the plot consists

almost entirely of this self-absorbed young aesthete's attempts to express his love to the levelheaded Anne Wimbush, Henry's niece. With his idealized view of women and his tendency to substitute literary phrases for feeling, Denis is a totally unlikely candidate for a lover. His unsuitability for the role becomes most evident when he is compared with Gombauld, his chief rival for Anne's attention. A scene illustrative of the way Gombauld acts out his passions while Denis merely mentally catalogues his depicts Denis sitting passively watching Anne and Gombauld dance, imaginatively describing them to himself as "moving together as though they were a single supple creature." Jealous of Gombauld's ardor, Denis consoles himself with the thought that despite his outward tameness he is a wild man inside; but he soon becomes caught up more in searching for a satisfactory phrase to express uncontrollable emotion than in actually experiencing it: "raging, writhing—yes, 'writhing' was the word, writhing with desire." Like the word "carminative" that Denis chooses more for sound than sense, the phrase has the right ring to it. However, it does not signify Denis's feelings, which are always more theoretically than actually passionate.

While Denis's inexperience as a lover is accentuated by the comparison with Gombauld, his intellectual immaturity becomes most evident in his encounters with Scogan. Only the narrator of the novel exceeds Scogan in ridiculing Denis's intellectual pretensions and romantic angst. And, at times, the two voices appear to converge. For example, when Scogan correctly infers that the novel Denis is writing deals with the artist-as-young-man idea, his voice blends with the narrator's (and Huxley's) in asking why "you young men continue to write about things that are so entirely uninteresting as the mentality of adolescents and artists?" The ironic joke here, of course, is that Huxley has made the mentality of the adolescent artist the subject of this novel.

Although Scogan and Gombauld are the yardsticks Huxley uses to mark Denis's intellectual and emotional shortcomings, it is Jenny Mullion, the enigmatic young deaf woman, who best captures the ironic contrast between the pose and the reality of Denis Stone. Her caricature of him, drawn from the scene in which he pretends to be oblivious to Anne and Gombauld dancing together, depicts the incongruities: "the expression of the face, an assumed aloofness and superiority tempered by a feeble envy; the attitude of the body and limbs, an attitude of studious and scholarly dignity, given away by the fidgety pose of the turned-in feet." Coming upon this drawing in Jenny's private notebook, Denis is jolted first into the realization that his defects are obvious to others and then into the recognition that there are consciousnesses other than his own. His usual tendency is to disbelieve that "other people should be in their way as elaborate and complete as he in his." Yet Jenny and her notebook, in representing to him "all the vast conscious world of men outside himself," make it apparent that the outer world exists and that it contains beings as intelligent and complex as Denis views himself to be.

This discovery constitutes the central moment of awareness for Denis in the novel, which has some elements of what Norman Friedman in "Forms of the Plot" calls the "education plot."[5] This kind of plot involves a change in the protagonist's thought or a shift toward a more comprehensive view. In *Crome Yellow*, Denis's education is never complete enough to effect much of a change in behavior; but once his egocentric view is shaken, he is compelled to take a somewhat wider outlook and at least to acknowledge momentarily the real and separate existences of those around him. He learns, as he expresses it in his overly

abstract way, that the "individual . . . is not a self-support-
ing universe. There are times when he comes into contact
with other individuals, when he is forced to take cogni-
zance of the existence of other universes besides himself."

The scene in which Denis conveys this new-found
truth to Mary Bracegirdle brings the two together at a point
in the novel when there is a significantly close correspondence between them. Experience has just made each of
them more aware of the complexities of human relationships, and they are both attempting to deal with these recent insights. Confronting his image in Jenny's notebook,
Denis has glimpsed that in any exchange with another person he is as much the perceived as the perceiver; and Mary,
seeking sexual experience as an antidote to "unnatural repressions," has found through her encounter with Ivor that
her emotions can become involved in the experiment.
Both Mary and Denis have had their narrow, analytical
view of relationship challenged, and their chance meeting
in the Crome gardens while they are in similar states of self-
examination and discovery presents an opportunity for
real communication between them.

It turns out, however, to be but one more illustration of
a theme running throughout the novel—that human beings
are "all parallel straight lines," never really connecting.
The conversation, which for heightened irony takes place
under the shadow of a statue of Venus, is contrapuntal.
Denis and Mary talk in a general way about the same subject—the problems associated with human contact—but
each pursues a different track. As a result, the conversation
becomes a series of brief, alternating monologues that follow independent lines of thought and never merge. Mary
dwells on the suffering inherent in intimate contacts, while
Denis, intent on maneuvering the discussion around so
that he can relate his experience with the notebook, par-
ries with a number of gambits about seeing one's self

through contacts with others. As is typical of him, Denis wants an audience; Mary, who is almost a match for Denis in her studied seriousness, wants to distance the unprecedented emotions her involvement with Ivor has brought into play. Under these circumstances, the conversation, like most of the others in the novel, turns into noncommunication. The encounter ends with the two walking in silence back to the house, having failed to make any sort of connection.

When Mary and Denis finally come to some understanding of one another, the consequences are unexpected and rather dismal for Denis. In a rare instance of mutual sympathy, they exchange confidences and commiserate over the pain of unrequited love. Denis confesses his "hopeless love" for Anne; Mary admits to feelings for Ivor. Relishing Mary's solicitude, Denis languishes, "embalmed" in the sympathy she offers him. But the more practical Mary prefers action to languor and persuades Denis that the only sensible solution to his problem is to leave Crome immediately. Under Mary's firm direction, Denis is propelled reluctantly along in a scheme to send himself a telegram that purports to summon him home on urgent business—until, finally, he finds he has no choice but to follow through with his departure. Making the arrangements, he feels as though he were preparing for his own funeral and decides: "This was what came of action, of doing something decisive. If only he'd just let things drift! If only . . . " Vowing never again to do "anything decisive," he passively accepts departure as his fate and climbs into the car (which he envisions as a hearse) waiting to carry him on a journey he does not wish to take.

The funereal note on which *Crome Yellow* ends serves principally as a comic exaggeration of Denis's plight; but it is also a fitting accompaniment to a somber tone that occasionally obtrudes upon the comedy in the novel and on the quietude of the Crome world. As Christopher Ferns appropriately observes, the "tone of *Crome Yellow* is, in places, almost elegiac."[6] It surfaces in Henry Wimbush's tale of his ancestor, Sir Hercules Lapith, a dwarf whose death stems from his inability to create a private world "proportionable to himself," and emerges especially in Wimbush's nostalgic reflections on the vanished glories and pleasures of the past. In lamenting "all the murdered past," Wimbush is largely out of tune with the other characters in the novel, who are either celebrants or exemplars of modernity. Even Mr. Scogan, Wimbush's companion representative of the older generation at Crome, is more enthusiastic about the future, which he envisions in terms of a scientifically induced "brave new world," than he is the past. However, Henry Wimbush's reflection on all that has been lost in the modern age, while not a predominant emphasis in the novel, sets modernism in historical perspective and, further, underscores Huxley's prevailing skepticism about the equation of progress with improvement.

Principally, the world depicted here has the brightness implied in the novel's title—chrome yellow being a color noted for its brilliance. Its inhabitants drift in and out of drawing rooms in search of amusement and pass the time in light flirtation and abstruse conversation. The horrors that Scogan refers to as "taking place in every corner of the world" are as remote from this country retreat as modern-day Crome is from the ancient monastery out of which it was built. Although Denis Stone tends to vex himself over life's complexities, his distress is more comical than serious. To his complaint that life is "horribly complicated" and renders one "horribly unhappy," Anne Wimbush delivers for Huxley the common-sense counter that makes apparent the incongruity of Denis's suffering in this pastoral setting: "Why can't you just take things for granted and as they come? . . . It's so much simpler."

Antic Hay

Aptly described by a 1923 reviewer as "half low comedy and half a genuine cry of despair,"[7] *Antic Hay* is both a more cynical and a more farcical novel than *Crome Yellow*. Huxley considered the novelty of the book to lie in its blending of "all the ordinarily separated categories—tragic, comic, fantastic, realistic"; and with this mixture of modes he depicts here a postwar world largely devoid of the values and ideals of the previous age. Focusing on a constellation of clever young sophisticates who find it "altogether *too* late in the day" for moral imperatives, he treats farcically the sexual license that stems from their denial of absolutes. In fact, much of the "low comedy" in the novel revolves around their bizarre sexual antics. At the same time, however, Huxley shows the tragic aspects of the postwar generation's subscribing to what years later, in *Ends and Means*, he calls the "philosophy of meaninglessness." With the word "dreams" no longer admissible, with love reduced to an equation, and with God dismissed as unprovable, the moderns of 1922 pictured here face a world in which futility is the ultimate reality and Nil—Nothing—the only omnipresent deity.

The mixture of tones and styles in the novel gives it something of a peculiar flavor. On the surface, there is the atmosphere of what Evelyn Waugh, Huxley's contemporary, calls "Henry James's London possessed by carnival."[8] Always in pursuit of pleasure, the young Bohemians seem to spend most of their time amusing one another with sophisticated repartee in the night-spots of jazz-age London or dancing from one sexual adventure to another. Part of the plot, which revolves around a series of ironic sexual pursuit and betrayal episodes, also contributes to the general impression the book gives of the twenties as a time of sexual liberation and revelry.

Yet beneath the carnival atmosphere runs an insistent undertone that speaks of the futility of these hedonistic pursuits. It finds a voice in the cabaret song "What's He to Hecuba?" in which the repetitive refrain "Nothing at all" emphasizes the emotional vacuousness of the pleasure-seekers. It is also represented symbolically in the lights of Piccadilly Circus, which offer only the "illusion of jollity"; and in the experimental beetles of Shearwater's laboratory that dart "uncertainly about, some obeying their heads, some their genital organs." Like the lights that "whizz round" and the beetles that dart about, the characters in the novel seem to be in perpetual but pointless motion. And at least for Theodore Gumbril, Junior, an ex-schoolmaster whose fantasy of freedom and fulfillment involves obeying his genital organs, and for Shearwater, the preoccupied scientist who ends up trying to escape the dictates of his, all the motion is a futile distraction that fails to bring happiness.

Gumbril and Shearwater are the two characters Huxley satirizes most directly for being Incomplete Men. Each in his own way exemplifies the imbalance that Huxley regards as a modern malady and that, ironically, he pinpoints in *Antic Hay* through the huckster hype of Mr. Boldero. In his advertising gimmick for pneumatic trousers, Boldero asserts that "already our modern conditions of civilization tend unduly to develop the intellect" and that "we're wearing out, growing feeble, losing our balance in consequence." Boldero, a capitalistic con man, makes an unlikely Huxley spokesman; but he hits, at least, on Shearwater's problem: he has developed his intellect at the expense of his passions. A physiologist "preoccupied with the kidneys," Shearwater methodically arranges his life for work by excluding the "absurd business of passion" and then is devastated when desire for Myra Viveash disrupts the arrangement.

In setting Shearwater up first as a type of the Incomplete Man who has managed to resolve the mind-body split through denial of his passions and then having him fall prey to them, Huxley makes some ironic plays on the idea of proportion. Initially, Shearwater is presented as a ponderous intellectual absorbed in science who has achieved a contentment of sorts through his one-sidedness. His notion of proportion is to make his work preeminent and everything else, including his marriage, subordinate to it. Convinced that "one can't have everything . . . not all at the same time in any case," he opts for work over love, the intellect over the passions. It is not surprising that his wife Rosie, whom he appreciates most when she intrudes least, looks elsewhere for attention and sexual satisfaction.

Shearwater's complacence vanishes after he falls under Mrs. Viveash's spell, and the intrusion of passion into his well-regulated life brings about a new insight into the meaning of proportion. He suddenly realizes that mind and body must be kept in balance—that one must render "unto Caesar the things which are Caesar's . . . and to God, and to sex, and to work" those things that are theirs. This coincides with Huxley's view that the integrated personality, or Complete Man, keeps spirit, flesh, and mind in proportion and in harmony. But Shearwater ultimately finds himself unable to act on his insight. He makes a start by admitting that he had been foolish to pretend immunity from passion and determining to discover more about Rosie, whom he had married as a "measure of intimate hygiene" and largely ignored. But his efforts are mistimed. In a scene providing one of the clearest illustrations of that perpetual disconnection endemic to the world of Huxley's novels, Shearwater attempts to draw closer to Rosie just as she is distancing herself from him. Dropping his characteristic detachment, he unexpectedly finds her detached. This reversal of roles and counterpoint of approach and retreat defeats Shearwater's tentative attempt to establish a meaningful connection with his wife. After this one overture, he withdraws and tries to work out in isolation his obsession with Mrs. Viveash.

The last chapter of the novel finds Shearwater alone in his experimenting chamber, pedaling furiously on a stationary bicycle "like a man in a nightmare." The scene takes on a surrealistic quality as Shearwater envisions Mrs. Viveash in pursuit and Gumbril's father, an architect who preaches proportion and has given it tangible form in a model of Christopher Wren's London, beckoning him to build his life with proportion. Trying to exorcise his desires, he holds onto the thought of proportion as though the idea itself has magical powers and persuades himself that with every turn of the pedal he is "working up the pieces of his life, steadily, unremittingly working them into a proportionable whole." The irony is that, while laboring desperately, Shearwater remains stationary. An absurd figure engaged in a fruitless experiment on a bicycle that goes nowhere, he epitomizes the futility that is a recurrent theme in the novel and exemplifies the failure of the Incomplete Man to achieve wholeness.

Theodore Gumbril, Huxley's other prominent Incomplete Man, presents a somewhat different case of disproportion. Like Denis Stone, Gumbril is fundamentally an idealist; unlike Denis, he does his best to quash his troublesome longing for the ideal by persuading himself that goodness and beauty are passé in the postwar world and by retreating into irresponsibility—playing the clown. His difficulty is predominantly that of reconciling spirit and flesh. Yet ironically, it is through Gumbril that Huxley introduces a version of the Complete Man—albeit a parodic version. Wishing to transform himself from the mild and melancholy individual that Myra Viveash calls "the weak, silent man," Gumbril dons a beard and pads out his physique to go in search of sexual adventure. He wants to take on the guise of the "complete Rabelaisian man": "great eater, deep drinker, stout fighter, prodigious lover; clear thinker, creator of beauty, seeker of truth and prophet of heroic grandeurs." This prototype of what Gumbril would like to become resembles Huxley's idea of the Complete Man; but the problem is that the bearded, bold lover Gumbril turns into is a sham—good for an afternoon of clandestine playacting with Rosie Shearwater—but otherwise a parody of the Huxleian ideal. In Gumbril's case, appearance and reality are as much at odds as flesh and spirit, and he never manages to reconcile either set of dichotomies.

Several of the other characters in the novel are also ironic parodies of sorts: Lypiatt, who sees himself in the tradition of titan artists such as Michelangelo, is simply a caricature of an artist; Mrs. Viveash, the novel's love goddess, is herself incapable of love; Coleman, the diabolist, is a reversed theist. The novel is full of fakes of one kind or another, all contributing to the impression the book gives of an age lacking in substance. But the principal focus of *Antic Hay* is on young Gumbril, an admitted chameleon, and his unremitting flight from responsibility. Through Gumbril, Huxley illustrates the idea expressed in the book that "every one's a walking farce and a walking tragedy at the same time." Gumbril's antics as he tries to overcome his natural passivity and do "something about life"—the affair with Rosie Shearwater, his attempts to promote pneumatic trousers—are a source of farcical humor. Yet at times Huxley shifts from comedy to treat seriously his protagonist's conscious rejection of the values and ideals that might give meaning to his life. In these moments, the tragedy of Gumbril's negation and consequent irresponsibility—the defeat of the spirit—overshadows the humor.

The two most significant instances of Gumbril's flight from accountability revolve around the only two women who ever seem to mean much to him—his mother and Emily, a shy young woman who evokes recollections of his dead mother. The opening chapter of the novel, which begins with Gumbril in the school chapel speculating skeptically on the nature of God, provides the first example and is also indicative of the way Huxley blends tones throughout the book. At first, Gumbril's impious thoughts, counterpointed with the Reverend Pelvey's sermon to constitute an ironic antiphonal response, set a comic tone; but this gives way to a more serious mood as the sermon triggers in Gumbril memories of his childhood and of his mother in particular. Nothing in the modern deprecation of the word "good," he realizes, can distort the fact that "she had been diligently good," and this recognition poses a problem for him. Wanting to rid himself of moral responsibility by denying moral consciousness, Gumbril asserts that the modern world is not just *beyond* good and evil but "merely below them, like earwigs." Yet the incontrovertible evidence of his mother's goodness augurs otherwise. Characteristically, Gumbril ignores the evidence. He makes a conscious choice to "glory in the name of earwig"—his declaration of freedom from responsibility—and throughout the novel this motto serves as a talisman to ward off the intrusion of anything too serious. When, for example, middle-aged Lypiatt rightly accuses Gumbril and his young cohorts of having no ideals, "no dream, no religion, no morality," Gumbril mockingly retorts: "I glory in the name of earwig. . . . One's an earwig in sheer self-protection." To be otherwise means being held accountable.

When Gumbril meets Emily, he is well launched into the sexual freedom he envisioned in deciding to leave teaching and to take advantage of "all chance encounters"—to live. However, Emily is no Rosie Shearwater, seduced as much by her own impersonations as by the men with whom she tumbles into bed. Emily, with her passion

for music and the beauties of nature, is genuine; and, for a
time, she elicits from Gumbril an uncharacteristic genuine-
ness in turn. For example, in Kew Gardens with her, Gumbril momentarily drops his typical sardonic patter and pos-
turing and speaks meditatively of the inward quiet the
modern world finds intolerable and, therefore, must dis-
turb: "There are quiet places also in the mind. . . . But we
build bandstands and factories on them. Deliberately—to
put a stop to the quietness. We don't like the quietness."

Gumbril sees the "crystal quiet" as a threat to his own
superficial way of life, realizing that without the diversions
"one would have to begin living arduously in the quiet,
arduously in some strange, unheard-of manner." His recognition of this uncharted path foreshadows, in some ways,
Calamy's mystical retreat into solitude in *Those Barren
Leaves*; but acknowledging the existence of a "crystal
world" outside the carnival is as far as Gumbril goes. Although Emily is native to this world, Gumbril prefers the
carnival, the life of diversion, in which it is simpler to sully
than to preserve beauty and purity. Once again, Gumbril
drowns out the call to accountability, thinking "how simple it was, too, to puddle clear waters and unpetal every
flower. . . . How simple to spit on the floors of churches!
. . . Simple to kick one's legs and enjoy oneself."

Despite his determination to opt for mindless pleasure,
Gumbril sometimes has to work at warding off the call of
the spirit. For example, when he attends a concert with
Emily, the Mozart music evokes thoughts of passion "pure
and unsullied" that he finds disconcerting. He first tries to
countermand them with the irreverent benediction he often uses to keep any hint of the ideal or the spiritual at bay:
"In the name of earwig. Amen." When that fails, he attempts to undercut the music, which he regards as deadly
"insecticide" for earwigs, by focusing on the physical ab-

surdity of the musicians. He notes the incongruity between the exquisite music and the beady-eyed, potbellied, sweaty men who have made it come to life. This undermining of the spiritual or aesthetic through the use of physical (and often scatalogical) grossness is a typical Huxleian technique. As Joseph Bentley observes of Huxley, "no one since Swift [has] so consistently manipulated a continuous parallel between exalted spirit and vile flesh."[9] Like Gumbril in this scene, Huxley is prone to work at convincing himself that the reality underlying the ideal is either sordid or ridiculous.

After a night of enchantment with Emily in which he experiences the happiness of a pure and mystical union, Gumbril finds negating the ideal increasingly complicated, but still manageable. Yielding to Mrs. Viveash's demand for company, he breaks his promise to meet Emily in the country and sends her a telegram claiming that he is a "little indisposed." Actually, Gumbril is a great deal indisposed—to commit himself to a relationship that calls for responsibility. Suppressing a twinge of guilt over his duplicity, he decides: "He was taking no responsibility for himself. It was the clown's doing, and the poor clown, poor creature, was *non compos*, not entirely there, and couldn't be called to account for his actions." He realizes that a relationship with Emily would necessarily be a "matter of integrity and quietness" and would require the arduous and unheard-of manner of living that he finds threatening; so he forfeits the relationship to play irresponsible clown.

Just as with the Mozart music, Gumbril undermines the beauty he has experienced with Emily to protect himself against having to admit that anything matters—to preserve his nihilism. Turned into a luncheon story for Mrs. Viveash's amusement, the innocent evening of enchantment with Emily becomes a "thrillingly voluptuous" episode and Emily herself a comic character in a tale about a

married virgin. Retelling the story of the "seduction" later
to Coleman, Gumbril realizes he has denigrated what had
been a moment of purity, an "eternal parenthesis" among
all his meaningless pursuits. But he shrugs off both the
relationship with Emily and his actions with the thought:
"Well, let everything go. Into the mud. Leave it there and
let the dogs lift their hind legs over it as they pass."

Gumbril's deliberate denial and irresponsibility cost
him Emily, whom belatedly he pictures as "perhaps the
one unique being with whom he might have learned to
await in quietness the final coming of that lovely terrible
thing" from which so often "ignobly he had fled." But the
recognition that he may have missed an opportunity for
happiness and genuine contact stalls him only briefly; then
he is in motion again in his continuous flight from responsibility and permanent attachments. In the last scenes of
the novel, he joins Mrs. Viveash, who also prefers running
along "parallel tracks" with people to connecting with
them, in a restless "Last Ride Together" before making
another escape—this time from England to the Continent
to sell his pneumatic trousers. With distraction as their
aim, they crisscross London, taking the city and its inhabitants as a spectacle for their own amusement. Their disconnection from everything and everyone comes across in
their speaking of going to "look at" Mercaptan, Coleman,
Lypiatt, and Shearwater as if these friends were the newest
version of the old Edgware Road peep shows.

Only once during this nighttime ride that Harold H.
Watts interestingly describes as a "Walpurgisnacht in
which the fires are not those of hell but the night traceries
of the electrical displays of Piccadilly Circus"[10] does Gumbril pause long enough to be overtaken by the quietness
and introspection from which he is fleeing. Most of the
visits he and Myra make during the evening are ironically
timed, or mistimed: They knock at Lypiatt's door while he

is contemplating suicide; catch Coleman with Rosie Shearwater; and peer at Shearwater in his laboratory while he pedals to escape from Myra. But when they visit Gumbril's father, a sweetly eccentric relic of a past age, it is Gumbril who is caught off guard. The revelation that Gumbril Senior has forfeited his treasured model of London for the benefit of an old friend momentarily arrests young Gumbril, whose whole pattern of life is in denial of such commitment and beneficence. His father's example challenges this denial and unleashes other reminders, which Gumbril has tried to suppress, of values he has rejected. All that connotes goodness and beauty to him—his mother, Emily, the music of Mozart—converge to confront him as he thinks:

Beyond good and evil? Below good and evil? The name of earwig. . . . The tubby pony trotted. The wild columbines suspended, among the shadows of the hazel copse, hooked spurs, helmets of aerial purple. The twelfth sonata of Mozart was insecticide; no earwigs could crawl through that music. Emily's breasts were firm and pointed and she had slept at last without a tremor.

Yet just as before, when he had reasoned that his mother's kind of goodness was not feasible for his generation, Gumbril dismisses the evidence of those values he wishes to negate. He concludes that "in the starlight, good, true and beautiful became one. Write the discovery in books— in books *quos*, in the morning, *legimus cacantes*." And with this determination that ideals are too ephemeral to be sustained in the light of actuality, Gumbril rejoins his waiting cab and is off again in his flight from commitment and from any hint that the world is other than meaningless.

Huxley wrote of *Antic Hay* in response to his father's negative reaction to the book that he intended it to reflect the "life and opinions of an age which has seen the violent disruptions of almost all the standards, conventions and values current in the previous epoch." As a mirror of the times, the novel pictures the uncertainty and restlessness of the rootless postwar generation; it also captures the prevailing sense of the pointlessness of everything through its lack of resolution. *Antic Hay* begins with Gumbril speculating about the "existence and the nature of God" and ends anticlimactically with his being taken in tow by Mrs. Viveash for yet another lap on their aimless journey. In between, Gumbril glimpses and rejects some vague other, more committed, way of living, and Shearwater tries and fails to gain proportion in his life; but there is no real indication in the book that they have much chance of finding a way out of the overwhelming accidie of the age. Futility and despair, Huxley suggests in this novel, are the inescapable consequences of the modern condition.

Those Barren Leaves

Less than a month after finishing *Crome Yellow*, Huxley already had plans to do a "gigantic Peacock in an Italian scene," as he describes his projected novel in a letter. Some three years later, in *Those Barren Leaves*, he returns to the house-party formula of eccentric people and clashing conversation in a central setting—this time gathering his British "oddities" in a palazzo amidst the hills of Vezza, Italy. As in *Crome Yellow*, the members of the assembled company are sufficiently diverse in age, perspective, and peculiarity to allow for the kind of ironic contrast Huxley likes to achieve by playing his characters off against one another.

The one character who stands alone as a consistently comic figure is Mrs. Lilian Aldwinkle, owner of the palace of the Cybo Malaspina and hostess to her fellow Britons. A faded beauty who imagines she has acquired Italian passion along with her Italian property, Mrs. Aldwinkle sees herself in her palace as "unofficially a princess surrounded by a court of poets, philosophers and artists." Among the entourage that her imagination promotes to greatness are Mary Thriplow, a governess turned novelist who laments being misunderstood by her readers; Francis Chelifer, a dilettante poet who edits *The Rabbit Fancier's Gazette* as a protest against art; Mr. Falz, a politician who in another era might have been a minor prophet; Lord Hoveden, a shy, lisping young nobleman who shows signs of daring only behind the wheel of his touring car; Irene, Mrs. Aldwinkle's niece and subject, who tries to be artistic for her aunt's sake; Calamy, an amorist who, at thirty-three, is in a muddle over his vacuous life; and Mr. Cardan, an aging hedonist who has been one of Mrs. Aldwinkle's lovers and whom she classifies among the "obscure Great." Mrs. Aldwinkle's salon may tend toward the second-rate, but she and her guests are the sort of "improbable people," as Huxley calls them, that make the comedy of this house-party novel decidedly first-rate. What has been described is Huxley's "little mocking devil,"[11] that satirical voice that can undercut a character or a scene with the mere turn of a phrase, is once more at play on the pretensions and posturings of a varied cast.

Although Huxley's facility for farce is as evident here as in *Crome Yellow* and *Antic Hay*, he seems more concerned in this novel that his reader recognize his underlying seriousness. In some ways, he is like Miss Thriplow, who wishes her readers to see in her novels "how serious it all is" beneath the comedy and the elegantly brutal satire. Yet the seriousness in *Those Barren Leaves*, rather than being an undertone, is essentially separate from the satire. This stems partially from Huxley's straightforward treatment of Calamy, whose struggle to give up pleasure seeking and find a new way to live forms the backbone of the book. Each time Huxley places Calamy at center stage, he shifts from satire to realism, and the "little mocking devil" momentarily retires. The result of these shifts is a curious segmentation in the book, which is further reinforced by Huxley's moving back and forth from third-person to first-person narration and his dividing the novel into distinct sections. After beginning in the section entitled "An Evening at Mrs. Aldwinkle's" with high-spirited Peacockian comedy, into which the serious presentation of Calamy's dilemma is but a brief incursion, and interjecting realism into the satire at intervals thereafter, Huxley finally veers away from satire altogether in the last pages of the novel to present Calamy's retreat from the world and new-found mysticism both realistically and with evident approval.

Thus, from a beginning not altogether different in structure and tone from *Crome Yellow, Those Barren Leaves* turns out to be the first of Huxley's novels in which the central character takes a decisive step in attempting to solve his problems. It is also the first in which Huxley suggests a solution to the modern dilemma of too much freedom and too few absolutes. As such, it contrasts sharply with *Antic Hay* and anticipates *Eyeless in Gaza* and other later novels. But unlike his approach in the later, more didactic fiction, here Huxley signals that the resolution he presents is but one of several possible. His central idea in the book, first voiced by Mr. Cardan and then taken up by Calamy, is that there are "eighty-four thousand different types of human beings, each with its own way of getting through life." And while Huxley sanctions Calamy's choice of mysticism as a way, he also tries to indicate not only that this route is simply one of "eighty-four thousand paths to salvation" but also that it is one particularly suited to Calamy's mood and circumstance.

Calamy is the kind of socially adept man of the world and successful gallant that Theodore Gumbril dreams of becoming. His adventurous past puts him at ease among men, and his self-admitted talent for "making love" gives him an insolent power over women. Yet from the moment of his arrival at Mrs. Aldwinkle's, it is apparent that he is in the process of some sort of transformation. He is both less absorbed with being *mondain* than Miss Thriplow expects and than, apparently, he once was. When Miss Thriplow, attempting to match the Calamy of her imagination with the man before her, admits that she had pictured him as "dazzlingly social," Calamy confesses: "Perhaps I was that sort of imbecile once . . . but now—well, I hope all that's over now."

Although evidently dissatisfied with his old habits and haunts and in a mood to live differently, Calamy is only in the first stages of his conversion from Casanova to contemplative. At this point, he recognizes the shallowness of his life as a Don Juan—even allows that it is "rather immoral"—but admits that his resolve breaks down before temptation. As he tells Mr. Cardan, the elder statesman of hedonism in the novel, he no longer likes "running after women" and wasting his time in the pursuit of "what is technically known as pleasure," yet he finds himself involved most of the time in just such occupations. Despite being what he calls "externally free," Calamy is enslaved by his passions and frustrated by his inability to break the bonds. In contrast to Gumbril, who wants to escape from responsibility into passion, Calamy wishes to escape from passion into responsibility—or, at least into some more "serious occupation" than seduction. But he has only the vaguest notion of what this new métier might be and no real confidence that present intentions will hold up against future temptations. In limbo between a way of life that increasingly seems futile and one as yet undefined, Calamy wonders "what's the way out?"

The novel traces Calamy's attempts to answer his question—to find a way out of the perpetual pull of the passions and to discover a more satisfying kind of life. But his is not a straight course. Some two weeks after confessing his disillusionment with love affairs, he is already philandering with Mary Thriplow. Partially, it is out of habit; it is also partially out of defiance. Calamy is at war with himself, and his trifling with Mary has less to do with sexual attraction than with self-assertion and distraction. One part of Calamy wants to change and knows that doing so would involve curbing the appetite for conquests; another part refuses to be bullied into changing and determines to persist in dalliance in defiance of what Calamy himself recognizes as the "most intelligent part of his own being." Thus Calamy's pursuit of Mary is a deliberate assertion of his right to "do what he damned well like[s]." At the same time, it is an attempt to quell the insistent voice urging him to find a more meaningful preoccupation. The affair presents a distraction through which Calamy tries to avoid having to think and, therefore, to confront some unfamiliar reality beyond the realm of his hedonistic experience.

As in *Antic Hay*, this other reality is represented here in terms of quiet. In the preceding novel, Gumbril, the Incomplete Man unable to balance body and spirit, finds the "crystal quiet" terrifying because it intimates the existence of truth and beauty outside the world of casual sex and jazz bands, and he knows that without the distractions he would be faced with living in some "strange, unheard-of manner." But Calamy, another Incomplete Man split between body and spirit, yearns for that unheard-of way of living suggested by the quiet even as he resists it. He envisions that if he were free of his enslavement to passion he would then have time to think and to "plumb the silences of the spirit." The problem is that desire interferes with thought, and thought inhibits abandonment to pleasure. Gradually, Calamy sees that he cannot satisfy body and spirit at the same time. Characterizing the conflict in terms of noise and silence, he recognizes that it is impossible for him to "lean out into the silences beyond the futile noise and bustle—into the mental silence that lies beyond the body" and simultaneously "partake in the tumult."

Yet before Calamy commits himself entirely to contemplation, he casts about for a middle way between hedonism and asceticism. He dreams of achieving some kind of "graceful Latin compromise" between the sensual and the spiritual in which both body and spirit could be cultivated. This is essentially the ideal of completeness that Huxley advocates elsewhere. His Complete Man is neither one-sided nor split but, rather, manages to keep all the elements of his nature in balance. But, through Calamy, Huxley is intent on exploring another definition of completeness. For example, when Calamy rejects the possibility of compromise and in a satiric tone very like Huxley's mocks the notion of pursuing the "Absolute" between supper and bedtime, it becomes apparent that Huxley is moving away from making the same kind of equation between completeness and proportion in this novel as in *Antic Hay*. There, he satirizes Gumbril and Shearwater for one-sidedness, measuring them against the standard of psychological harmony in which body, mind, and spirit are all rendered their appropriate due. Here, through his serious presentation of Calamy's quest for transcendent reality, Huxley suggests the possibility of a unity beyond that of body, mind, and spirit—a unity achieved only through overcoming the limitations of the body.

Ironically, Calamy's intuition of that unity begins with a recognition of separateness. In one of the novel's key scenes, Calamy's thoughts distract him from his seduction of Miss Thriplow, and he begins to concentrate on his hand, reflecting on the several different "modes of existence a thing has." For example, his hand exists variously in the physical world as a collection of cells or as a force-field of atoms; it is also an object of mind; and it has moral significance as an instrument of good and evil. This idea that, as Calamy phrases it, things "exist simultaneously in a dozen parallel worlds" is one that fascinated Huxley for most of his lifetime. He articulates it in "The Education of an Amphibian" when he asserts that "simultaneously or alternately, we inhabit many different and even incommensurable universes." But his interest goes beyond charting the separate modes of existence and on to the more intriguing question of the relationship between the different modes of being, and in *Those Barren Leaves* he explores the question through Calamy. Thus, from the realization that universe lies upon universe, each layer separate and distinct, Calamy proceeds to look for the connection between the parallel worlds. Resolving to burrow through the layers by "thinking really hard," he hopes to discover the mysterious unity behind the apparent separateness.

His search for a unity discernible only to the meditative eye leads him to dissociate himself from society and retire to the mountains to contemplate. All of that which follows—his enforced celibacy, his vague mystical notions, and especially the obvious symbolism of his removal to a mountaintop—is the stuff of which Huxley's satire is usually made. But there is little hint of satire or irony here. Mr. Cardan and Chelifer pay a visit and play the role of antagonists, raising many of the objections to Calamy's mystical path to salvation that might be expected of Huxley himself; but although Calamy flounders occasionally in trying to counter their arguments, Huxley never actually undercuts him. Near the end of the novel, he does reveal Calamy's self-doubts, but this has the effect of rendering him more human than absurd. Further, Huxley concludes the novel on what is for him at this point an unprecedented note of hopefulness. Just as Calamy begins to brood over the loss

of his old familiar life and to think he may have been foolish to take up this strange new one, he finds a consoling
sign in nature. In the vista below, the limestone crags at
sunset take on the semblance of a "precious stone, glowing
with its own inward fire," and Calamy thinks: "Perhaps he
had been a fool. . . . But looking at that shining peak, he
was somehow reassured."

The description of limestone crags reaching through
the clouds into the sky and Calamy's finding validation in
this natural scene of his decision to concentrate on the
mystery, the "ulterior reality" beyond the world of appearances, are calculated to recall Wordsworth's "Tintern
Abbey," where the romantic poet finds in the harmony of
landscape and sky an emblem of universal unity and affirms the possibility of seeing "into the life of things."
What appears to be a Wordsworthian resolution is uncharacteristic of Huxley and surprising in view of his criticism of
Wordsworth's philosophy in essays such as "Wordsworth
in the Tropics" (*Do What You Will*) and "A Wordsworth
Anthology" (*On the Margin*). It is also at odds with
the satire of "Wordsworthian formulas" that infuses the
"Fragments from the Autobiography of Francis Chelifer"
section of the novel and that crops up at intervals throughout the book. As Robert S. Baker has recognized in his
study of the link between historicism and romanticism in
Huxley's novels, *Those Barren Leaves* can be viewed within the context of Huxley's condemnation of the "underlying aesthetic and epistemological assumptions"[12] of romantic poetry.

Huxley was particularly bothered by Wordsworth's
tendency to systematize—to erect a cosmology out of emotions and to endow a landscape with metaphysical meaning. While admitting that Wordsworth possessed the "poet's gift of seeing more than ordinarily far into the brick
walls of external reality," Huxley faults him for using his

gift in the service of philosophy—for simplifying the "impersonal diversity" and mystery of nature to suit his preconceived theories. And it is on this issue of the inherent mysteriousness of nature that Huxley subtly goes against Wordsworth in the ending of *Those Barren Leaves* even as he contrives there to evoke Wordsworth's poetry. Significantly, the last lines of the book, although hopeful, are inconclusive. Calamy does not find in nature that "something far more deeply interfused" of Wordsworth's "Tintern Abbey," which Huxley equates with the god of Anglicanism. Neither does he discover any particular correspondence between man and nature or come to see nature as anything but impersonal and separate. Rather, he simply finds nature "beautiful, terrible and mysterious," a symbol of some unknown "formidable reality," and it is this evidence of mystery that reassures him of the rightness of his quest.

Although Calamy's spiritual struggle and conversion constitute the main subject of this digressive novel, Huxley is ultimately more interested in exploring the various ways that different types of people deal with life than in advocating a particular method for doing so. His early description of *Those Barren Leaves*, written while the book was still in process, indicates that he meant it to be a "discussion and fictional illustration of different views of life." Thus the idea that there are many individualistic ways to go about building what Huxley refers to in "Wordsworth in the Tropics" as a "metaphysical shelter in the midst of the jungle of immediately apprehended reality" recurs throughout the novel. Mr. Cardan makes the point in maintaining that "every man has his own recipe for facilitating the process of adaption" and Calamy in asserting that "each man can achieve salvation in his own way." But the illustration of the varying philosophical possibilities lies with the characters themselves, each of whom has his or her own definition of reality and recipe for adapting to it.

For the sentimentally romantic Mrs. Aldwinkle, art is the reality that justifies existence and comes closest to deifying man; but being singularly lacking in the "power of self-expression," she surrounds herself with people from whom she hopes to hear the one "apocalyptic thing that she had been waiting all her life to hear." At the other extreme, Chelifer, whom Calamy rightly calls a "reversed sentimentalist," has acquired all the literary accomplishments but insists that art is a "lying consolation," a false ideal that should have been tossed overboard along with religion and patriotism. Constructing a metaphysical shelter out of the notion that the "deepest of all realities" is human stupidity and that it is better to confront this truth than to seek escape in the falsehood of idealism, he deliberately takes up his station in Gog's Court—the "navel of reality"—where he commits himself to the tedium of editing a livestock trade paper and gloats over the horrors of the world around him. Chelifer insists that he is a realist and takes great pains to emphasize his repudiation of both the oracular romanticism of his father, an "ardent Wordsworthian," and his own previous romantic idealism. But, as Robert S. Baker has observed, Chelifer is actually a "reverse romantic" of the sort that Huxley describes in "The New Romanticism."[13]

In this essay, Huxley characterizes modern romanticism as being simply the "old romanticism turned inside out, with all its values reversed." Individualism and idealism are replaced by collectivism and materialism; art, although still practiced, is regarded as irrelevant. From Huxley's perspective, the new reverse romantics are "as extravagant and one-sided . . . as the Romantics themselves," but they lack the redeeming quality of erring in their extravagance on the side of the soul and the individual. This exaggerated one-sidedness is sketched into Huxley's portrayal of Chelifer, whose attempt to devote himself to the "exclusive concentration on the relevant" entails the denial of individual imagination and spiritual awareness.

The irony of Chelifer's situation is that he rejects one philosophy for its lack of inclusiveness and chooses another even more restricted. In renouncing romanticism because it fails to account for human insipience, he embraces a philosophy that disregards man's capacity for creativity and spirituality. One scene in the section of the novel entitled "The Journey" especially illustrates this negation. In Rome with Mrs. Aldwinkle and several of her guests, Chelifer points out to his companions the cupola of St. Peter's designed by Michelangelo—at once a symbol of the spiritual and the creative. But to Chelifer both the spiritual significance of the dome and the creative genius of Michelangelo are irrelevant, and he dismisses them with one sentence: "But what has it or he to do with us?"

Mr. Cardan's response to Chelifer in this scene provides a clear indication of his governing view of life. While assenting to Chelifer's cynical perspective of reality, he would prefer to include art among the amusements—such as wine, "learning, cigars and conversation . . . religion for those that like it, sport, love, humanitarianism, hashish and all the rest"—that help man adapt to his circumstances. The hedonistic Cardan sees life as a farce in which "it is only the acting that matters" and to which the most suitable response is to indulge "in all the pleasures."

Like Chelifer, Cardan maintains that it little serves to think too much about one's situation; but where Chelifer recommends a general unawareness as a safeguard against disillusionment, Cardan tries to avoid thinking specifically about death "lest it should spoil his pleasures." He is made to confront mortality with the death of Grace Elver, a harmless idiot whom he intended to marry for her money, but this has the effect of merely confirming him in the view that the body rather than the spirit is the principal element in the human drama. At Miss Elver's bizarre funeral, Cardan concludes that the body is the "one appalling fact" because gradually the spirit succumbs to the flesh and, in the end, all that is left is the "doomed, decaying body." Cardan's growing obsession with the decrepitude of old age and the inevitability of death becomes apparent later as he challenges Calamy's retreat into meditation with the point that no amount of contemplation can explain away the "fact that, at the end of everything, the flesh gets hold of the spirit, and squeezes the life out of it." Despite this somber preoccupation, the conclusion of the novel finds Cardan preparing to move on to Monte Carlo with Mrs. Aldwinkle in search of diversion. His way of "getting through life" is to indulge in all the pleasures and creature comforts someone else's pocketbook can afford while trying to forestall the denouement of life's tragedy as long as possible.

Of all the characters, Mary Thriplow is the most chameleon-like and, thus, in one sense, the most adaptable. Her facility for taking on the coloration of her immediate environment and the quick changes she makes as she interacts with the various members of the house party are a recurring source of comic satire in the novel. Huxley focuses on her protean transformations not only to set the comic tone of the opening chapter but also to illustrate one of the book's final points: that the choice of a particular path to salvation must be individualistic and suited to a person's own "peculiar talent." On this point hinges his justification of Calamy's decision to cultivate his talent for meditation by becoming a contemplative and also his harshest satire of Miss Thriplow. For as Miss Thriplow, at bedrock an emotionally sterile intellectual, turns mystical

under Calamy's influence, she illustrates the absurdity of
trying to appropriate someone else's idea of reality and of
adaptability taken to the extreme. Already divided between a fabricated, much-desired emotional self and a genuine analytical nature, each encapsulated in the separate
journals she keeps, she becomes farcical in her attempt to
take on spirituality too. Her effort to give the spirit "its fair
chance" by thinking hard about God, like her ritualistic
struggle to evoke emotion by recalling her cousin Jim, fails
when analysis overtakes sensitivity.

Miss Thriplow is among those she labels "hypocrites
of instinct"—people who simulate emotion (and, in her
case, also spiritual awareness) with their minds. In assum-
ing the guise of spontaneous Wordsworthian or contemplative Christian, she tries to belie the truth of her fundamental nature. But her negation is ultimately less extreme than
Cardan's and Chelifer's. Both of them base their lives on
denial: Cardan on a denial of death, and Chelifer on a
denial of life outside the "dustbin" of sordid reality.
Against such abnegation, Huxley sets Calamy's affirmation
of an "ulterior reality to be looked for"; and although the
search involves Calamy's discarding the social and sexual
baggage of his former life, it represents a movement toward
something rather than a retreat from a reality he fears to
confront.

The "barren leaves" of this novel are those who seek
refuge in metaphysical shelters erected out of fear. Mrs.
Aldwinkle's romantic religion of love stems from her fear
of growing old; Miss Thriplow's reverence for spontaneous
feelings arises out of anxiety over her emotional aridity;
Cardan's hedonism is an attempt to stave off the "unexhil-
arating theme" of death; and Chelifer's nihilism is an escape from failed idealism. In contrast, Calamy's mysticism
is an adventurous step into the unknown. Rejecting the
safe but sterile "surface-life of appearances," he opens up

to the possibility of glimpsing the reality behind the "cosmic illusion"; and although the outcome of his mystical exploration remains uncertain at the conclusion of the novel, the positiveness of the ending tends to validate Calamy's conviction that "it's not fools who turn mystics."

Point Counter Point

According to Mark Rampion, the character who preaches the ideal of balance and completeness in *Point Counter Point*, mystics are not merely fools but lunatics and perverts in a world so out of kilter that it is an "asylum of perverts." So, too, are the intellectuals, the aesthetes, the Don Juans, and every other kind of lopsided specialist who denies a part of his human nature. As the proponent of life and the prophet of doom for twentieth-century civilization in this novel, Rampion decries the modern disease of self-denial, which he calls "Jesus's and Newton's and Henry Ford's disease," and of which asceticism (and its mirror image, promiscuity), science, and mechanization are symptomatic. The cure he prescribes for a sick society in which men are already "three quarters dead" from having sacrificed their humanity to pursue God, abstract theories, money, or their prurient imaginings is a change in the individual psychology of modern man.

As Rampion views it, such a change will involve the modern's recognizing what the Greeks long before him knew—that balancing and harmonizing the conflicting elements of human nature is requisite for sanity and health. It will entail his attempting to live as a "real complete human being." The ideal Complete Man, says Rampion, is a "creature on a tight-rope, walking delicately, equilibrated, with mind and consciousness and spirit at one end of his balancing pole and body and instinct and all that's unconscious and earthy and mysterious at the other."

Since this doctrine of Rampion's is the core philosophical position of *Point Counter Point*, it is clear that in this novel Huxley has moved away from the point of view he sustains in *Those Barren Leaves* with his approbation of Calamy's mystical conclusions. He says in one of his letters that the "main theme" of *Those Barren Leaves* is the "undercutting of everything by a sort of despairing skepticism and then the undercutting of that by mysticism." In *Point Counter Point*, he undercuts mysticism with Rampion's gospel of consummate humanity, the central tenet of which is to live fully as man instead of killing off a part of the self in attempting to be more than human.

This shift in perspective coincides with Huxley's renewed friendship with D. H. Lawrence in the mid-twenties and reflects Lawrence's influence on Huxley's thinking about the problem of those "diverse laws" of human nature that cause self-division. In what Huxley labels Lawrence's "ethical principle," which is "that a man's first moral duty is not to attempt to live above his human situation," Huxley found the grounds against the sort of one-sidedness he had been satirizing. As he argues in *Do What You Will*, where he extends and refines some of the ideas in *Point Counter Point*, intellectualism and asceticism are attempts to be "superhuman"; and the "means by which men try to turn themselves into supermen are murderous." Further, and most significantly, Huxley found in Lawrence's vision of the whole man a solution to the problem of both one-sidedness and self-division. The Lawrentian ideal of equilibrium, or what Harry T. Moore calls "balanced conjunction" between flesh and spirit,[14] becomes Huxley's ideal of "balanced contradictions." Unlike the lopsided superhumanist and the disjointed split man, the Complete Man, as Huxley envisions him, both admits the equal right to existence of all the contradictory elements of his nature and manages to keep them in harmony—or, at least, in a state of "balanced hostility."

Although this standard of wholeness is held forth and, to some degree, exemplified in *Point Counter Point* through Rampion, whom Huxley modeled largely on Lawrence, the novel is predominantly a study in fragmentation. Of the more than twenty characters comprising Huxley's unusually extensive dramatis personae, all but a few are drawn specifically to demonstrate some particular facet of incompleteness. For example, among the circle closest to Rampion, who functions as arbiter in this "novel of ideas" wherein each person's character is implied in the ideas for which he is the mouthpiece, Philip Quarles represents the imbalance of intellectuality, Maurice Spandrell that of reversed spirituality, and Denis Burlap that of emotionality. Quarles, who has some of Huxley's own characteristics, is a novelist whose "cool indifferent flux of intellectual curiosity" makes him at home in the world of the mind but a foreigner in the realm of emotion and human contacts. Spandrell is a "reversed ascetic," a profligate that hates sex, and also a kind of inverted diabolist who through debauchery and, finally, murder tries to conjure God from his "abstract absolute lair." Denis Burlap, through whom Huxley presents a scathingly satiric portrait of writer John Middleton Murry, is a proponent of emotional spirituality who churns up his feelings at will and uses his ethereality as a tactic to seduce women into a sort of spiritualized, disembodied lovemaking. As Jerome Meckier points out, the main reason for Huxley's "assault on Murry-Burlap" was what Huxley saw as "Murry's lack of emotional balance."[15] Thus, in delineating the character of Burlap, Huxley represents him as a split man whose spirituality and sexuality reflect his excessive, adolescent emotionalism.

Rampion brands Quarles an "intellectual-aesthetic pervert," Spandrell a "morality-philosophy pervert," and Burlap a "pure little Jesus pervert" and claims that the world is full of their types—"all perverted in the same way—by trying to be non-human." The assortment of other characters in the world the novel portrays bears out his notion of the pervasiveness of deviance from the central norm of full humanity. For example, among those of the younger generation, the ménage à trois of Marjorie Carling, Walter Bidlake, and Lucy Tantamount form an interesting pattern along the continuum of non-human incompleteness. Marjorie stands at the extreme of "bloodless spirituality" and Lucy at the other extreme of emotionless carnality. Where Marjorie prefers the *idea* of love to lovers and their bestial passions, Lucy opts for sex and a succession of lovers in lieu of either the idea or the reality of love. Walter, a Shelleyan romantic who believes in spiritual, ennobling love but falls prey to what he regards as his "beastly sensual desires," is caught between the two women.

More critically, however, he is caught between the spiritual and the sexual demands of his own nature. For even after he gives up on the affair with Marjorie and takes Lucy as his mistress, thus succumbing to his carnal cravings, he has not resolved the conflict between spirit and flesh. Ashamed of his sensuality and wanting to justify it in the name of something higher, he tries to make his relationship with Lucy fit his idealistic dream of love; but Lucy's amused detachment and insistence on disengaging love from sex shatters his dream, leaving him unjustified and guilty.

Lucy Tantamount, as the foremost proponent of postwar modernism in the novel, is intent on throwing overboard such excess baggage as romantic love. Like the young people in *Antic Hay*, she believes that "living modernly's living quickly" and pursues diversion without emotional entanglements. But in contrast to *Antic Hay*, where disproportion seems mainly a condition of youth, *Point Counter Point* depicts not only the postwar generation as off balance but also their parents. There is no parent here speaking for proportion, as Gumbril Senior does in *Antic Hay*. Instead, there are only prototypes of one-sidedness such as Lord Edward Tantamount and John Bidlake.

A scientist who experiments with regeneration in newts, Lord Edward is reminiscent of Shearwater in his absorption with the abstruse and is a prime example of Rampion's "fossils of the future"—intellectuals that, as he describes them, are as "disproportioned as any diplodocus" because they have sacrificed "physical life and affective life to mental life." At the other end of the spectrum, artist and sensualist John Bidlake has sacrificed the spiritual and mental for the physical life. Huxley generally presents him more sympathetically than Lord Edward, perhaps because Bidlake's worship of the body has some characteristics of Rampion's "phallism"; but by concentrating most of the plot line devoted to Bidlake on the physical decline of this once "Gargantuan" voluptuary, Huxley also shows the vulnerability of the exclusively sensual life to its prime nemeses: illness and old age. Having dedicated himself in both his art and his life to the flesh, the aging painter faces the loss of his powers bereft of consolation. He and Lord Edward have each in different ways denied "half the facts" in their one-dimensional preoccupations.

The two dozen or so largely disproportioned characters in *Point Counter Point* are elements in what Huxley calls the "human fugue." They interact in various combinations, producing momentary harmony or discord, but each remains essentially alone and separate. Although the musical analogy is new in this novel, whose title suggests the interplay of note against note, the idea that people are disconnected from one another and live as "parallel straight lines" is inherent in each of Huxley's previous nov-

els. Often in the house-party books it is expressed comically as Huxley satirizes the egotism separating one person
from another; in *Antic Hay* it is presented more seriously
as a pervasive symptom of the age. With *Point Counter
Point*, Huxley adds a new dimension to the problem of
isolation by focusing on a far greater number of familial
relationships than in the earlier novels and showing that
the difficulty in making human contact is as acute among
parents and children and husbands and wives as among
casual acquaintances at a country house or a London ca-
fé —and far more serious. There are three generations of
Quarleses in the book and two of Tantamounts and
Bidlakes, but there is not a single instance of communion
among the various family members. At best, the parents in
these distinguished, upper-class families take an intermit-
tent interest in their children, although mostly they ignore
them benevolently. For their part, the children tend to accept the parents' existence with a "touch of amused resig-
nation," as Philip Quarles does his father, or to find them,
as Lucy does, droll "but hardly possible."

The same sort of separation exists in most of the mar-
riages. And, surprisingly for a writer who includes the
man-eating female among his standard repertoire of wom-
en characters, Huxley places much of the blame for this
lack of connection on the husbands. John Bidlake's irresponsibility, Sidney Quarles's resentment of his wife's superiority, Philip Quarles's emotional remoteness, and Lord
Edward's sexual and emotional immaturity are all recog-
nizable barriers to successful marital relationships. With
each of these men except Sidney Quarles, the inability to
make or to sustain connection in his marriage stems from
the very one-sidedness that keeps him from being a fully
integrated personality. For example, Lord Edward and Philip are as undeveloped emotionally as they are overdevel-
oped intellectually, and their rather abstract and distanced

approach to love drives their wives to seek fulfillment in other relationships. At the opposite extreme, Bidlake has Rabelaisian appetites but little regard for the constraints of marriage, and his lack of commitment causes Janet Bidlake to retreat into the private world of her imagination. Interestingly, he is depicted positively as a lover and negatively as a husband. When contrasting Bidlake's and Lord Edward's sexual relationships with Lady Edward, Huxley calls him a "healthy sensualist." In portraying him as a husband, he shows him to be an irresponsible rake. Like Gumbril in *Antic Hay*, Bidlake runs from any arrangement likely to impose responsibilities, preferring to live "emotionally and socially speaking, from hand to mouth."

The only man in the novel that has a successful marriage is Mark Rampion, the exemplar of wholeness. He and his wife Mary complement one another and are equally strong partners in a relationship of mutual support. By nature an uninhibited "noble savage," Mary has shown Rampion how to live instinctively, shocking him into confronting and unlearning the puritanism of his childhood. In turn, he guides her through the nuances of social interaction, interpreting other people's motives and characters for her. Theirs is a marriage of give and take—boisterous, quarrelsome, and, unlike any of the other relationships in the novel, accented by laughter. In contrast to the other couples, whose enervating relationships lack the direct contact of either quarrels or laughter, the Rampions are not afraid to risk confrontation or to resolve the combat by laughing at themselves. The dynamics of their straightforward and vigorous relationship become evident in the scene at Sbisa's Restaurant, when the two are introduced. Characteristically, Rampion is complaining as the episode begins, and Mary is laughing and countering his complaints with her typical atavistic gusto. They launch into a full-scale verbal sparring match, punctuated with exaggerated threats of physical violence, and end up bursting into laughter.

The same pattern of verbal warfare resolved through laughter recurs in the final scene of the following chapter, which recounts their courtship and early years of marriage. Both scenes illustrate the vitality of the communication between the Rampions. Rather than running along parallel tracks, never making contact, they crash head-on and come out of the collision more intact as a couple than ever. As Spandrell observes after witnessing the incident at Sbisa's: "Each separately was good; but together, as a couple, they were still better."

The Rampions' relationship points up the various deficiencies of all others in the novel. Their commitment contrasts with both Lucy's and Spandrell's promiscuity, their intimacy with the alienation of Walter and Marjorie, and their sexual maturity with Burlap's and Beatrice's repulsive sexual puerility. But the clearest and apparently most intentional contrast is between the Rampions' forthright communication with each other and Philip and Elinor Quarles's inability to make direct contact, despite the deterioration of their marriage and the growing distance between them.

Huxley introduces the Quarleses and the problem of their "parallel silences" concurrently, deftly establishing their separateness by charting their private and distinctly different thoughts as they both gaze at the moon. Prone to think in impersonal abstractions, Philip associates the moon with "three-formed Hecate" and then becomes absorbed in a far-ranging intellectual reverie. The more emotional Elinor is reminded of the moon that shone on her Hertfordshire garden in the earlier, romantic years of her marriage. The ensuing scene, in which Elinor attempts to provoke some personal response from Philip, is an obvious counterpart to that in which the Rampions fight it out and end up laughing—except with the Quarleses there is no give and take and no resolution. Like Mary Rampion, Elinor asks her husband, "Where would you be if I left you?" But in contrast to Rampion, Quarles is unresponsive, retreating into the self-protective silence that separates him even further from Elinor.

Since Elinor is alone in making the effort to bridge the distance between her and Philip, the responsibility for the failure in communication lies largely with Quarles, whom Huxley sets up as a foil to Rampion not only in the wrong-headedness of his philosophy but also in his inadequacies as a husband. The deficiencies in both arenas stem from the same source—from the kind of pervasive, relentless intellectualism that Rampion calls "non-human." Even Elinor, who often sounds like Rampion, tells Philip that he is "almost human" and that in his effort to understand intellectually the emotions he does not feel he is "like a monkey on the superhuman side of humanity" trying to "feel down" with his intellect. This emotional void in Quarles, coupled with his tendency to entrench himself in silence whenever Elinor tries to break down the barriers between them, essentially precludes any communion in the marriage. Instead of being healthily combative like Rampion, Quarles is repressively civilized and detached—to the point that when Elinor finally stops trying to make contact with him and becomes "unnaturally silent," his only response is to turn the conundrum of their relationship into a possible fictional plot.

Subjecting his personal problems to the novelist's detached scrutiny, Quarles writes in his notebook that it might be "rather interesting" to concoct a character who lives mainly on the "abstracted intellectual plane" and to dramatize the discord in his relationship with his wife, who lives principally through her emotions and intuitions. He envisions this fictionalized version of himself recognizing his own psychological defects and desiring, in theory, to change; but, like his creator, this character would be unable to turn theory to fact. As an earlier notebook entry reveals, Quarles has come to see, through Rampion's influence, that his intellectualism is a substitute for living and an escape from emotional involvements. Theoretically, he can define what must be done if he is to change, for as he writes: "The problem for me is to transform a detached intellectual skepticism into a way of harmonious all-round living." But, in reality, he finds the lifelong habit of encouraging his "intellectualist tendencies" at the expense of emotions and human relationships too ingrained to give up—and too pleasurable an escape. Thus, he retreats from the idea of foregoing the simpler intellectual pleasures for the complexities of life by deciding that he may be naturally predisposed to coldness and a preference for abstractions.

Having determined that he (and the character projection of himself) may well be "congenitally incapable of living wholly and harmoniously," Quarles essentially abdicates responsibility for making any changes or trying to save his marriage. In his plot outline, he notes that the wife threatens to leave the husband for a "more human lover," which, of course, corresponds to Elinor's threatening to leave him for Everard Webley. He then resolves the problem, at least, fictionally, by observing that "she is too much in love with him to put the threat into effect." Despite his wishful thinking, the problems in his real-life marriage remain unresolved. In one of those ironic juxtapositions characteristic of his style in *Point Counter Point*, Huxley undercuts Quarles's perspective with the next sentence: "That Sunday afternoon Elinor and Everard Webley drove down into the country." Ironically, while Philip is relying on Elinor's love to keep their relationship together, she is giving up on reaching him and resigning herself to having an affair.

The plot dealing with the deterioration of the Quarleses' relationship is but one of several in the novel involving some aspect of degeneration. In structuring *Point Counter Point* along the lines of the process he terms the "musicalization of fiction," Huxley develops a number of "parallel, contrapuntal plots" designed to provide a variety of modulations on a theme. His intention is to duplicate in fiction the rich and complex pattern of music in which there are shifts from one mood to another as a theme is stated, developed, altered, and restated. Although Huxley does not entirely succeed in transferring the techniques of one artistic medium to another, he does manage to imitate in the novel the musical effect of continuity within variety by having his several plots play variations on the same theme. And that overarching theme is the degeneracy of, and within, the modern age. Each of the major plot lines—Spandrell's attempt to conjure God through evil and violence, Philip's failure to change from spectator to actor, Burlap's pseudo-spiritual seduction of Beatrice, the dissolution of several sets of relationships, John Bidlake's physical decline, paralleled by the death of little Phil—contributes its part to the overall impression the novel gives of diminution, disintegration, and decline. There is no positive progression in the book—only the spiraling, downward movement into a kind of inferno in which, ironically, the hypocritical Burlap is the modern-day Dante and a romp in the bathtub with Beatrice the equivalent of paradise.

Behind the particular illustrations of degeneracy within the modern age lies the general notion of the twentieth century itself as a degeneration from past eras. Rampion provides the foundation for this idea in equating lopsidedness with barbarism and completeness with civilization and in maintaining that mankind has been on a course of steady decline into barbarism since the Greeks. His drawing showing two outlines of history, one according to H. G. Wells and the other from his own perspective, gives the concept symbolic representation. For example, in illustration of the Wells view of history as progressive, the drawing is composed along the lines of a crescendo. A small monkey is succeeded by a slightly larger pithecanthropus, which is succeeded by a larger Neanderthal man, and the size of the figures continues increasing through the ages and on into "Utopian infinity." Rampion's version of history follows a similar crescendo movement up to his depiction of a very large Greek, after which the stature of his representative men begins to decline until, eventually, they are distortions. The Victorians are small and misshapen. Twentieth-century man is an abortion.

Huxley reiterates this idea of a decline in social and human development since the Greeks in *Do What You Will*. In these essays, he blames the regression mainly on monotheism and Christian spirituality and advocates a "new religion of life" designed to accommodate the diversity that these doctrines exclude. For his example of such a life-enhancing religion, he turns to the vitalist humanism of the Greeks. He suggests that the Greeks worshipped life in all its inconsistencies and accepted human nature as they found it. Recognizing that "man is multifarious, inconsistent, self-contradictory," they lived "multifariously, inconsistently, and contradictorily." As a consequence, Huxley believes, they were incomparably more complete than modern man, whose survival depends upon his cultivating his humanity.

By the final essay in this collection, Huxley is declaring himself a "life-worshipper" and implying that it is possible for men of his generation to achieve the wholeness requisite for salvation. Such optimism is absent from *Point Counter Point*, which, as George Woodcock has observed, is "indeed a strange book to have been written by a man who at this period was presenting himself in his essays as a devotee of life worship."[16] The novel offers little hope that modern man will regain the balance of his Greek predecessors; for despite Rampion's preachments about the possibilities of living integrally, the picture presented in this book is of the failure of the moderns to live either psychically or socially integrated lives and of the "infantilism and degeneracy" that are the fruits of this failure.

Lacking the broad humor of *Antic Hay* or the positive resolution of *Those Barren Leaves, Point Counter Point* is, as Huxley admits in one of his letters, a "rather frightful novel." Certainly, it is the most violent of his 1920s novels. In between the lover's quarrel that opens the book and the scene of infantile sexuality that ends it, there are four deaths, one of them a brutal murder and another the prolonged and tortured death of a child from meningitis. This seemingly gratuitous violence drew from D. H. Lawrence the accusation that Huxley only thrilled to "murder, suicide, and rape."[17] But Lawrence's "splenetic complaint,"[18] as Sybille Bedford terms it, does less to call attention to the truly frightful nature of the novel than his rather complimentary observation that Huxley managed to present in *Point Counter Point* an accurate rendition of the "state of man as it is."[19] For while Rampion represents man as Huxley thinks he ought to be, Philip Quarles, Spandrell, Burlap, and the several other warped and fragmented characters represent man as Huxley thinks he is. It is this grim view of the human condition that makes *Point Counter Point* a particularly alarming novel.

In the four novels published between 1922 and 1928, Huxley surveys essentially the same scene—the world of the postwar intelligentsia—but with a "multiplicity of eyes" as Philip Quarles calls the fictional technique of subjecting a single reality to several different perspectives. Quarles describes Huxley's intention when he speaks of wanting to look at things with "all those eyes at once," that is, wanting to show how reality looks when seen simultaneously from the standpoints of science, art, religion, and other such particular slants. Fascinated with the variety of aspects under which any event or reality can be considered, Huxley concentrates in these novels more on point of view than plot or character. In fact, plots are slight and several of the characters reconstituted from book to book, but the working out of points of view is careful and intricate.

By rendering an event in terms of different "eyes," Huxley intends to show something of the simultaneous existence in parallel worlds that he considers fundamental to reality. As he asserts in an essay in *Music at Night* entitled "And Wanton Optics Roll the Melting Eye," we spend our lives "first in one water-tight compartment of experience, then in another"; but the artist can "break down the bulkheads between the compartments and so give us a simultaneous view of two or more of them at a time." Viewed in this way reality looks "exceedingly queer," he suggests, and that is "how the ironist and the perplexed questioner desire it to look." From *Crome Yellow* through *Point Counter Point*, Huxley assumes the stance of the ironist, juxtaposing points of view and breaking down the bulkheads between the compartments of experience in order to show, as Quarles puts it, "the astonishingness of the most obvious things."

3

Heaven and Hell:
The Utopian Theme
in Three Novels

The notion of a utopia, whether conceived of as an earthly paradise on the order of Eden or an ideal state such as Plato's Republic, is a dream of balance and perfection. It presupposes a condition better than that in which man may presently exist. The antithesis of the utopian dream is the anti-utopian or dystopian nightmare—a vision of a world more flawed and frightening than the one in which man lives at the time. Throughout Western thought, these two contrary conceptions have run parallel, the utopian heaven counterbalanced by the dystopian hell. Their histories constitute what Frank and Fritzie Manuel in *Utopian Thought in the Western World* very expressively describe as a "landscape of chiaroscuro."[1]

Within a span of thirty years, Aldous Huxley wrote three novels predicated on the utopian theme that cast a similar pattern of light and shade. The first two, *Brave New World* (1932) and *Ape and Essence* (1948), are sketched in the dark tones of the dystopia. They are meant not only to illustrate Huxley's conviction at the time that the "Utopian way leads to hell" but also to serve as a warning of the dangers of undiscriminating faith in technological progress. In contrast to these futuristic fables about life in a post-cataclysmic world, *Island* (1962) is set in the present and exhibits a positive picture of a society that succeeds where the one portrayed in *Brave New World* fails—in balancing the rights of the individual and the community. In fact, in a 1958 television interview, Huxley described *Island* as a "kind of reverse *Brave New World*"; and to emphasize his hope for the realization of the ideal society depicted in the novel, he calls the book a "Topian rather than a Utopian phantasy, a phantasy dealing with a place, a *real* place and *time*, rather than a phantasy dealing with *no* place and time."[2] In this his final work of fiction, Huxley offers his vision of what the world *might* be if it underwent a fundamental shift in philosophy.

Brave New World

Brave New World has been regarded as the archetypal dystopia[3] and as the "most influential anti-utopian novel of the twentieth century."[4] At the time he was writing the book, Huxley thought of it as a difficult piece of work—a novel on the "horror of the Wellsian Utopia and a revolt against it." Earlier, in *Point Counter Point*, he had satirized Wells's view of an inevitably progressive future; in *Brave New World* he sets out to show what a future that is the culmination of certain aspects of the twentieth century would be like. Projecting, for example, the results of this century's fascination with science and with mechanization into "Utopian infinity," he imagines a future in which human beings are scientifically engineered and mass-produced as easily and with as much standardization as one of Henry Ford's automobiles. Purely from the standpoint of efficiency and stability, this world of A. F. (After Ford) 632 represents an advance over the one Huxley is trying to warn; but in terms of freedom and full humanity, it is a version of the hell that Huxley, through Rampion in *Point Counter Point*, predicts as the outcome of industrialism and Americanization. Such a hell materializes, as Rampion foresees, "in the name of science, progress, and human happiness."

Brave New World depicts a society shaped by science and technology. Thus, to introduce his readers to that society of the seventh century, Huxley concentrates initially on the main scientific factors at work in fashioning it. The most important of these is the "manufacture" of human beings designed perfectly for their predestined social functions. Beginning with the fertilization process, differentiations are made that will determine whether the eventual human specimen turns out as an Epsilon sewage worker or an Alpha world controller. Those ordained to be Betas and Alphas, the skilled workers and the intelligentsia of this highly stratified society, are not only the products of biologically superior ova and sperm but are also given the best prenatal treatment. Those fated for the lower orders undergo "bokanovskification," a process by which a fertilized egg is arrested in its development, subjected to X rays and alcohol, and thereby made to produce anywhere between eight and ninety-six embryos. The standard Gammas, Deltas, and Epsilons resulting from this application of the principles of mass production to biology make up the bulk of the labor force and are also the most important contributors to the stability of the World State because they are the most easily controlled. Having either limited or almost no intelligence, the members of the lower castes can be counted on to perform the most mindless tasks without boredom and without giving their superiors trouble.

Through such a systematic practice of eugenics and dysgenics, the World Controllers lay the foundation for their goal of social stability. Human reproduction (or production) is no longer left to chance as in the "pre-modern" days of fathers and mothers and viviparous procreation. Now, life is genetically engineered in the laboratory and the embryos carried to term in bottles on conveyor belts until "decanted" into what is ironically termed "independent existence."

Added to this biological determinism is the equally crucial process of social conditioning, which ensures that each person adapts to and actually prefers his predestined role to all others in society. As the Director of the London Hatchery and Conditioning Centre explains, the "secret of happiness and virtue" is "liking what you've *got* to do. All conditioning aims at that: making people like their unescapable social destiny." To this end, the conditioning starts with the embryo as, for example, the future chemical worker is trained to tolerate toxins and the future inhabitant of the tropics is taught "from the bottle" to abhor cold. Later, the child's mind is not only made to concur with the body's predisposition for heat or chemicals but is also shaped to think his destiny the best of all those possible. This is accomplished through the technique of "hypnopaedia," or sleep-teaching, in which the state repetitively sends the sleeping child the suggestions that are eventually to constitute all his beliefs. Working on the principle that "one believes things because one has been conditioned to believe them," those who regulate the society manipulate the minds of their charges in the interest of stability and happiness and create a populace that would not (and, generally, *could* not) think things should be otherwise.

Occasionally, despite the elaborate mechanisms of conditioning and the means employed to keep people happy—the distribution of the drug *soma*, the encouragement of sexual promiscuity, the orchestration of Solidarity Services in which *soma* and sex are the key elements of religious ritual—there arises discontent among the ranks. Being more individualistic genetically and less restrictively conditioned than their fellows, the Alphas are the most susceptible to disaffection. They have the acumen to realize that the World State's manufactured brand of happiness is at the expense of freedom and, sometimes, one of them begins to wonder what it would be like if he were free. The plot of *Brave New World* deals with two such men, both Alpha Pluses, who feel alienated from their society and, additionally, with a real outsider from another culture, who opens the door to freedom for one of them.

Huxley moves slowly into plot in this novel, devoting the first two chapters to an explanation of the principle mechanisms of social control: eugenics/dysgenics, neo-Pavlovian conditioning, and hypnopaedia. A great deal of exposition is required to locate the reader in this strange world of the future, and Huxley handles it deftly through the device of a guided tour in which the various functions of the London Hatchery and Conditioning Centre are detailed for a troop of students. Along with the students, the reader follows the guide through the several factory-like rooms in which conveyors unceasingly move forward with their "load of future men and women."

In the third chapter, Huxley introduces Mustapha Mond, Resident Controller for Western Europe, and shifts to a montage technique of rapidly alternating scenes. Mond, the only character in the novel with a thorough knowledge of history (despite his assertion of the Fordian dictum that "history is bunk"), carries the exposition in this chapter. His function here is twofold: first, to recount the historical context of the World State; second, to contrast the present with the past, which he attempts to do in such a way as to make conditions before the advent of the World State seem undesirable. Alternating with his exposition are scenes in which the Hatchery's off-duty workers prepare for the diversions they have been conditioned to enjoy. Their talk of going to the Feelies or to play Obstacle Golf or of "having" a new sexual partner is juxtaposed for ironic effect with Mond's recitation of the horrors of the past. While he tells of the "appalling dangers of family life" in the age when there were mothers and fathers and sexual exclusiveness, the workers discuss the need to become more promiscuous in order to be seen as conventional; for in this new era, "every one belongs to every one else" according to the hypnopaedic proverb, and nonexclusiveness is the norm.

It is through the conversations taking place in the workers' dressing rooms that two of the leading characters and the plot begin to come into focus. Lenina Crowne, an especially "pneumatic" Beta who is clearly the product of the culture and her class, is discussing with her friend Fanny (also named Crowne) her plan to interrupt a four month's stint with only one lover by accepting Bernard Marx's invitation to visit a Savage Reservation. Simultaneously, in another changing room, Bernard Marx listens resentfully to a discussion of Lenina Crowne's sexual attributes as one man recommends her to another. Marx's reaction is partially jealousy and partially resistence to the rules of promiscuity. More dimunitive than his Alpha Plus status would dictate, he envies the men of his caste their assurance and unself-conscious superiority—their success at having as many women as they want. At the same time, he is alienated enough from the social system to be slightly revolted by the normal practice of nonexclusive, impersonal sex. He sees Lenina's carefree sexuality as a degradation and wishes for something now considered taboo: a relationship founded on emotional intimacy.

In a society that insists on divorcing sex and emotion, Lenina is well adjusted. It is Bernard who is maladjusted. He is another of Huxley's eccentrics, but, ironically, his peculiarities are those of a sane man. The problem is that he lives in an insane world. His penchant for solitude and his preference for reality over *soma*-induced unreality make him suspect in this topsy-turvy society that prizes the community more than the individual and happiness more than truth. But the real sign of his unorthodoxy is his interest in cultivating his emotions. Like many of Huxley's characters, Bernard is emotionally infantile; however, in his case it is the result of cultural conditioning and a requirement of social conformity. So when he tells Lenina that he wants "to know what passion is" and "to feel something strongly," he is consciously rebelling against the system that allows some of its subjects to be adults intellectually but requires them to be "infants where feeling and desire are concerned."

Yet for all his brave talk and little acts of defiance, Bernard is not a hero and poses no real challenge to the system. Like Denis Stone, Theodore Gumbril, and other of Huxley's boastful but indecisive protagonists, Bernard is not up to the task of living as "an adult all the time," as he puts it. However, he and his friend Helmholtz Watson, whose superior mental ability also sets him apart, serve a critical function in the first half or so of the novel in being the only dissenters against the order of things.

In addition, Bernard functions as the avenue through which Huxley introduces into the narrative the single perspective that is completely contrary to those prevalent in the World State—the point of view of the Savage, whose unique culture has been concocted from Indian primitivism and Shakespearean sophistication. Once the Savage takes over the role of providing the antithetical perspective, Huxley can largely dispense with Bernard as a dissenting voice. In the last portion of the book, Marx becomes an increasingly unsympathetic character and the object of scathing satire. For example, when his role as guardian of the Savage gives him unprecedented prominence, his dissatisfaction with society dissipates. As the authorial voice of the novel satirically states: "Success went fizzily to Bernard's head, and in the process completely reconciled him . . . to a world which, up till then, he had found very unsatisfactory."

Even if Bernard were more inclined to keep up his resistance, he and Helmholtz can only go so far because their conditioning has created boundaries they cannot cross. As Mustapha Mond explains, "each one of us . . . goes through life inside a bottle." An Alpha's bottle may be, relatively speaking, enormous, and within it he may have a sense of autonomy; but he still has limits confining him. Only someone from outside the culture and its conditioning can present, if not a challenge, at least a complete contrast. The Savage from the New Mexico reservation represents that contrast. As Peter Firchow observes in his *The End of Utopia*, the appearance of the Savage in the new world "brings about the confrontation of the individual natural man with the artificial society of unnatural men."[5]

Huxley's use of a savage as his principal critic of the civilization crafted through science has the effect of recalling Rousseau's Noble Savage and the whole context of the romantic idealization of the natural man. The reminder turns out to be mostly ironic, however, since Huxley is unprepared to follow the romantic primitivists in asserting the innate goodness of man; nor is he convinced that urbanity is particularly bad. He does share the romantic's suspicion of progress, and it is such a suspicion that prompted the writing of *Brave New World*. But the central irony in Huxley's evocation of the Noble Savage idea is that although John Savage, as he comes to be called, fits the romantic prototype in that he has a natural dignity and intelligence, he is not a savage.

Born in the wilds of New Mexico, the progeny of parents with origins in the new world, the Savage lives as a stranger among the Pueblo Indians. Although he tries to join the Indians in their tribal rituals, his white skin and

blue eyes accentuate his difference, and he is excluded
from the life of the reservation. This isolation from the
primitive culture, plus his thorough grounding in the
works of Shakespeare, account for his being in many ways
more civilized than the inhabitants of the new world.

Naturally, the Savage is also set apart in his nobility
from the Indians, whom Huxley does nothing to romanti-
cize. If anything, he exaggerates the squalor in which they
live and the brutality of their superstitions. As Huxley depicts it, the reservation embodies the horrors of past ages
that Mond describes earlier in the novel—the filth, decrepitude, disease, death, sexual possessiveness, and familial
perversions. Its one advantage is that it allows for the freedom to suffer and to be unhappy.

An outcast in primitive society, the Savage enthusiastically accepts Bernard's invitation to return with him to the
"Other Place," which he has idealized from scraps of stories his mother has told him of the civilized world. He
greets the prospect of going to London with Miranda's
speech in the fifth act of *The Tempest*:

> O, wonder!
> How many goodly creatures are there here!
> How beauteous mankind is! O brave new world
> That has such people in't! (V.i.181–84)

Like Miranda, the Savage is an innocent and unaware of
the irony in this remark. Unlike Miranda, he eventually
discovers the irony as he sees the discrepancy between the
description and the reality to which it refers. But in this
initial utterance of hope and joy, the Savage is as oblivious
to Bernard's undercutting question "Hadn't you better
wait till you actually see the new world?" as Miranda is to
Prospero's more matter-of-fact statement "'Tis new to
thee" (V.i.185).

Subsequent repetitions of the "O brave new world" refrain serve as something of a gauge of the Savage's reaction to civilized life. Joyful expectation turns to disgust as he encounters the "wonders" of an educational system that teaches the Malthusian Drill (for the correct application of contraceptives) and Death Conditioning and forbids Shakespeare; of the "Feelies," a sensory cinematic experience in which the audience can not only see a rather pornographic modern-day rendition of *Othello* called *Three Weeks in a Helicopter* but feel the stereoscopic kisses; or of the identical Bokanovsky Group workers that, conditioned to be dwarfed and deformed, staff the factories. Yet despite his growing sense of the irony of the Shakespearean litany, which he repeats almost unconsciously, he resolves to hold fast to his childhood vision of the paradisiacal Other Place. His attempt to separate the ideal and the real works until the death of his mother, when he is forced to face the devaluation of the individual in the new society. This realization is brought about first by the blasé reaction of the schoolchildren to Linda's death and, second, by John's confrontation with science's tribute to uniformness, the Bokanovsky Group—or, in this case, two groups of eighty-four identical Deltas each. The horror of such sameness and stupidity breaks into the Savage's consciousness, and the inappropriateness of his involuntary "How many goodly creatures are there here" makes a mockery of his idealism.

To this point, Miranda's speech has served to express joy and wonderment, to trigger childhood memories of paradise, to mock the Savage's idealism. Its final function is as a challenge and an affirmation of the possibility of transforming the world the Savage sees as hell into the utopian heaven of his dreams. That shift from derision to challenge takes place as he watches the distribution of *soma* to the Deltas and thinks:

"O brave new world, O brave new world . . . " In his mind the singing words seemed to change their tone. They had mocked him through his misery and remorse, mocked him with how hideous a note of cynical derision! Fiendishly laughing, they had insisted on the low squalor, the nauseous ugliness of the nightmare. Now, suddenly, they trumpeted a call to arms. "O brave new world!" Miranda was proclaiming the possibility of loveliness, the possibility of transforming even the nightmare into something fine and noble. "O brave new world!" It was a challenge, a command.

The Savage responds to the challenge by hurling the Delta's daily ration of *soma* out the window and berating them for their infantilism. For although he proclaims freedom as his mission, compassion quickly turns to hatred for the witless creatures he has come to save. He is joined in the ensuing melee by Bernard, who hesitates on the fringes of the battle in an "agony of indecision," and Helmholtz Watson, who plunges enthusiastically into the fracas with the Deltas and the police in gas masks and actually seems to be set free by this act of self-determination.

The farcical nature of this scene, with Helmholtz and the Savage punching away at the howling Deltas and Bernard running about under the pretense of helping, contrasts sharply with the succeeding major episode, in which the three renegades are confronted by the Controller, Mustapha Mond. Their different reactions reflect their fundamental differences in character. Learning that he may be exiled to an island populated by others who have exhibited antisocial tendencies, Bernard pleads obsequiously on his own behalf, blaming everything on Helmholtz and the Savage. While Bernard seems to have shrunk in stature, Helmholtz appears to have grown. He speaks to the Controller with assurance and earns his respect when he requests that the island to which he is exiled have a "thoroughly bad climate." As a writer intent on exploring the

possibilities of his creativity, he chooses a bracing climate
in the belief that it will stimulate his imagination. The novel leaves the impression that his banishment to the Falk-
land Islands will turn out to be the making of this would-be
poet.

Even more than Helmholtz, the Savage meets the Controller confidently, and his ability to engage in a debate
with Mond as an intellectual equal sets him apart from his
supposedly more civilized companions. The dialogue between the two of them is the raison d'être of this episode,
which takes up two chapters. Through their conversation,
Huxley focuses on the central problem that *Brave New
World* is set up to explore: the extent to which happiness
must necessarily exclude freedom and to which freedom
must include unhappiness. The new-world civilization is
predicated on the conviction that happiness and freedom
are mutually exclusive and that happiness is the greater
good. To prove the benefits of such an assumption, Mond
points to the positive aspects of his society—it is stable and
peaceful; its citizens are safe and happy, free of the deleterious effects of passion, unfulfilled desires, old age, and
disease. When questioned more directly by the Savage
about the place of art, science, and religion in the society,
Mond explains that these have been sacrificed in the interest of comfort and happiness! Instead of high art, there are
the Feelies, the scent organ, and synthetic music; instead
of scientific inquiry, there is scientific orthodoxy; instead
of religion, there are the Solidarity Services. Beauty, truth,
and God are incompatible with machinery and universal
happiness, but, Mond contends, so are evils such as decrepitude, disease, and the fear of death.

The Savage does not reject the notion that an uncon-
trolled society will incorporate these evils; he simply
chooses freedom, even with its attendant pain, over happiness without freedom. To the Controller's observation that

in the new world they "prefer to do things comfortably," the Savage responds: "But I don't want comfort. I want God, I want poetry, I want real danger, I want freedom, I want goodness, I want sin." Mond points out to him that, in fact, he is "claiming the right to be unhappy," as well as the right "to grow old and ugly and impotent; the right to have syphilis and cancer; the right to have too little to eat; the right to be lousy; the right to live in constant apprehension of what may happen to-morrow; the right to catch typhoid; the right to be tortured by unspeakable pains of every kind." The Savage holds firm: "I claim them all."

This simple and noble line would have been a fitting conclusion to *Brave New World* had Huxley wished to assert the superiority of primitivism over scientific determinism, but that is not the case. Mond has the last word in the debate, responding to the Savage's declaration with a shrug and a detached "You're welcome." Further, in the final chapter, Huxley makes the Savage's brand of primitive religion, which involves abasement and self-flagellation for purification from sin, seem particularly ferocious and unappealing. Thus, he effectively undercuts any temptation the reader might have to give primitivism the edge. And as if to remove any doubt that what he has presented is, basically, a choice between two evils, the last scene in the novel is of the Savage, dead by his own hand, swinging like a compass from the ceiling of an abandoned lighthouse.

Fifteen or so years later, Huxley felt that the Savage's being offered "only two alternatives, an insane life in Utopia, or the life of a primitive in an Indian village, a life more human in some respects, but in others hardly less queer and abnormal" was a defect in the novel. In his foreword to the 1946 Collected Edition of *Brave New World*, he indicates that at the time the book was written he found both amusing and possibly true the idea that

"human beings are given free will in order to choose between insanity on the one hand and lunacy on the other."
But between the early thirties and the mid-forties, Huxley
came to believe in the possibility of sanity; and in the
foreward, he projects the kind of community that might
result from devotion to this ideal. He says that the community's economics "would be decentralist and Henry-Geor-
gian, politics Kropotkinesque and co-operative. Science
and technology would be used as though, like the Sabbath,
they had been made for man, not (as at present and still
more so in the Brave New World) as though man were to be
adapted and enslaved to them. Religion would be the conscious and intelligent pursuit of man's Final End, the unitive knowledge of the immanent Tao or Logos, the transcendent Godhead or Brahman." This outline of a utopian
society takes on form and substance a decade and a half
later in *Island*.

Ape and Essence

Huxley's foreword to *Brave New World* was written
after Hiroshima and the demonstration of the immense
capacity of atomic power for destruction. In it he predicts
that unless man blows himself and his planet "to smither-
eens," the utopian horror of *Brave New World* might well
be realizable within a century. Since his attention in this
piece is focused on the conditions that could conceivably
lead to the sort of world described in the novel, it is not to
his purpose to deal with the other possible eventuality—
that of a third world war in which, through the use of
nuclear weapons, man very nearly manages to destroy the
human race. With *Ape and Essence*, published two years
later, he takes this possibility as his subject, depicting in
grotesque detail the mutant society that springs up in the
aftermath of nuclear war.

Huxley organizes *Ape and Essence* along the lines of a fiction within a fiction. The introductory, outer narrative begins in January 1948 on the day of Gandhi's assassination—a historical moment that symbolizes the defeat of nonviolence as an avenue of social and political progress. Half a world away from the shooting in India, two Hollywood screenwriters provide ample illustration of the observation made later in the novel that "tragedy is the farce that involves our sympathies, farce, the tragedy that happens to outsiders." One of them, the unidentified narrator of the first twenty or so pages of the book, who thinks remarkably like Huxley, understands both the symbolism and the tragedy of Gandhi's death. His sympathies are engaged to the point that he includes himself among the "believers in Order and Perfection" ultimately responsible for killing Gandhi and construes the murder as an act symbolic of society's rejection of the "only possible means to peace." The other writer, Bob Briggs, is more preoccupied with his own messy personal affairs, which he elevates to the level of romantic tragedy, than with the events in distant India. He sees himself as "all the Romantic poets rolled into one," but his talent for trivializing the serious and magnifying the mundane makes him more fit for the Hollywood film industry, whose superficiality Huxley satirizes here.

Against the backdrop of the failure of passivism and the vacuousness of Hollywood life, Huxley moves toward the horrific vision of a future world to which, he implies, these earlier conditions contribute. When Briggs and the narrator discover a rejected movie script among a load of manuscripts destined for the incinerator, they go in search of William Tallis, its author. They learn of his recent death and enough of the facts of his life to deduce that the horrors of World War II and, perhaps, his guilt over having abandoned a wife and child in Germany account for his ghastly picture of a world given over to evil. Whatever his reasons, Tallis envisions a time when Belial, "Lord of the Flies," is in control and works his demonic will upon the remnants of a race that has regressed from a human to a simian state. His script, entitled "Ape and Essence," records that vision and constitutes the bulk of Huxley's novel.

In moving from the opening story to Tallis's script, Huxley shifts from realism to fantasy and from straightforward narration to a scenario format that mixes action, narration, directions for camera angles, and other techniques used in movie shooting scripts. He apparently had some initial reservations about this format, for, as he indicates in a letter to Philip Wylie, he tried at first to write *Ape and Essence* "straight," but the "material simply wouldn't suffer itself to be expressed at length and in realistic, verisimilitudinous terms. The thing had to be short and fantastic, or else it could not be at all. So I chose the scenario form as that which best fulfills the requirements."

It was a form with which Huxley was by that time well familiar. He had worked on at least two film scripts for major studios in the late thirties and early forties. The advantages it offers for a novel like this one are several: the technique of dissolving from one scene to another allows for the kind of juxtaposition Huxley likes to use for ironic effect; the camera directions focus the reader's attention on a variety of details, thereby making this a much more graphic presentation of the material than it might otherwise have been; and the voice-over narration gives Huxley a perfect vehicle for the ironic commentary he favors and a rationale for the "set pieces"—passages in which the important ideas are laid out. Huxley admits in his letter to Wylie that one of the difficulties he has in his writing is in "combining ideas with narrative." That problem is somewhat mitigated in *Ape and Essence* through the scenario format and the use of the narrator to set the stage, interpret and describe action, shift the scenes, and articulate (sometimes in verse) most of the major ideas.

The controlling idea in the novel comes from the lines in Shakespeare's *Measure for Measure* from which Huxley took his title:

> But man, proud man,
> Dress'd in a little brief authority,
> Most ignorant of what he's most assur'd
> (His glassy essence), like an angry ape
> Plays such fantastic tricks before high heaven
> As makes the angels weep. (II.ii. 117–22)

The point of the passage is that men trying to act like gods make as ludicrous (and pathetic) a spectacle as apes imitating men. Huxley uses this notion in his indictment of scientists, whose attempts to play God have ushered in the age of Belial and thereby condemned man to animalism. But he also goes beyond Shakespeare's analogy to suggest that in forfeiting his humanity man does, in fact, become the ape, the brutish part of his nature. As the narrator states in an early poetic commentary: "Only in the knowledge of his own Essence / Has any man ceased to be many monkeys." Thus the central dichotomy of the novel is that of ape and essence, the bestial and the uniquely human aspects of man's nature. In knowing and living in accordance with his "glassy essence"—his fragile yet spiritual humanity—man has a chance of survival; in forgetting his nature, he reverts to the ape.

The narrator makes the contrast between ape and essence explicit in the latter portion of the book when he says: "Love, Joy and Peace—these are the fruits of the spirit that is your essence and the essence of the world. But the fruits of the ape-mind, the fruits of the monkey's presumption and revolt are hate and unceasing restlessness and a chronic misery tempered only by frenzies more horrible than itself." The world of the twenty-second century depicted through Tallis's script is the product of the ape mind—of men dissatisfied with the given order and ignorant of their essence, who played fantastic tricks with their scientific inventions and ended up destroying civilization.

The society that emerges out of the dust cloud of the atomic bomb pays obeisance to Belial as the originator of the destruction and evil, for as its leaders reason, only the Devil would "desire the degradation and destruction of the human race." In describing what Satan has wrought by planting the diabolical ideas of progress and nationalism in men's minds, Huxley intends to shock. Images of degradation and death abound. In California, worst hit by the holocaust, the survivors mine the cemeteries for their clothing, stoke the communal ovens with books from the public library, and fashion drinking cups out of skulls. A huge sewer stands as the remaining relic of the glory and grandeur of the defunct civilization. More horrifying than these images of the wasteland world, however, are the purification ceremonies on Belial Day in which deformed children are sacrificed while the populace engages in an orgy of mating during this one time of the year in which sex is permissible. The sacrifice of blood for the propitiation of sin—in this case the sin of having produced a mutant monster—is, of course, a parody of the Judeo-Christian emphasis on blood atonement. Huxley pushes the parody to its limits by describing in gruesome detail the ritualistic infanticide done in the name of religion.

As in *Brave New World*, where the Solidarity Service is a parody of the Eucharist, Huxley mocks both Christianity and its Satanic counterpart. Here, too, a frenzy of group sex serves as the culmination of the religious ritual. Against the backdrop of the antiphonal chanting of Belial's priests that it is time "for the Baboon to be master," the worshipers tear off one another's aprons emblazoned with the word "NO" and couple madly during the short rutting season. These are the victims of gamma rays, which have changed men's sexual patterns. As the narrator explains: "Thanks to the supreme Triumph of Modern Science, sex has become seasonal, romance has been swallowed up by the oestrus and the female's chemical compulsion to mate has abolished courtship, chivalry, tenderness, love itself." Only a small minority of the population has escaped this conditioning and is inclined to follow the old-style mating pattern; but these "Hots," as they are called, are the oppressed minority, for any socially unregulated behavior such as falling in love is punishable by death.

Ironically, the plot of Tallis's script (and thus the inner narrative of Huxley's novel) is a love story. It involves a sexually repressed botanist, Dr. Alfred Poole, called by his students and colleagues "Stagnant Poole," and a young inhabitant of the mutant culture named Loola, whose only sign of her heritage is an extra pair of nipples. Poole is a member of the New Zealand Discovery Expedition that lands on the coast of Southern California in the year 2108 in a schooner christened the *Canterbury*. Like the Savage in *Brave New World*, he is a throwback to an earlier phase of civilization—one particularly at odds with the sexual practices of the society in which he is a stranger. But the Savage, having imbibed from the Indian culture and from Shakespeare strict views of love and chastity, kills himself when he succumbs to desire and engages in the ritualistic orgies of the new world; for Poole, participation in the purification revelries of the new society sets him free from his inhibitions and allows him to love.

When Poole meets Loola, he is a Freudian case study in repression. A shy mother's boy who sees sex as a sacrilege, he has spent half his life plagued by erotic fantasies and guilt, torn between adolescent desires and "maternal pre-

cepts." Since he has not dared direct his desire to a particular woman, his yearnings have in some ways been as indis-
criminate as Loola's; and hers are the seasonal frenzied
impulses of oestrus, which she becomes compelled to satisfy with any partner available. These two for whom love
and sex are mutually exclusive seem an unlikely couple to
carry the positive message in this otherwise totally grim
novel, but they become the vehicles through which Huxley
asserts the possibility of personal wholeness amidst the
fragmentation of a world that has been blown to smither-
eens. Out of the animalistic Belial Night mating, which
Huxley renders satirically obscene by choreographing to
the sound-track accompaniment of the Good Friday music
from *Parsifal*, Poole and Loola both discover a new dimension to sexual relationships. For Poole, it is romantic love;
for Loola, it is monogamy. As the narrator explains in one
of the novel's best stylistically balanced passages: "And so,
by the dialectic of sentiment, these two have rediscovered
for themselves that synthesis of the chemical and the personal, to which we give the names of monogamy and romantic love. In her case it was the hormone that excluded
the person; in his, the person that could not come to terms
with the hormone. But now there is the beginning of a
larger wholeness."

Except for a few side turnings to add to the already-
lengthy list of twentieth-century conditions that led to Belial's takeover, Huxley focuses the remainder of the novel
on the couple's separateness from the rest of the society
and their increasing transformation into this larger wholeness. Poole, the timid "introverted sexualist," becomes
forceful and decisive once he centers his passion on Loola
and reconciles sensuality and spirituality. Surprisingly,
Poole's transformation is traceable in terms of his reading
and recitation of Shelley, a poet whom heretofore Huxley

has negatively associated with too idealistic and ethereal a kind of love. For example, in *Point Counter Point*, Rampion calls Shelley a "mixture between a fairy and a white slug" in a diatribe against bloodless, spiritual love, and the novel supports his point of view. In addition, Walter Bidlake is satirized for his idealistic attempt to model his life with Marjorie Carling on the Neo-Platonic precepts of Shelley's "Epipsychidion." But in *Ape and Essence*, Huxley describes with evident approval Poole's emergence from the darkness of surreptitious sexual yearning into the light of a romantic love that leads from the sensual to the spiritual. Quoting from "Epipsychidion," Poole calls Loola a "mortal shape indued / With love and life and light and deity" and an "image of some bright Eternity," thus associating her with the Shelleyan ideal of beauty, the function of which is to cause the lover to ascend from the lower realms of flesh to the higher realms of spirit.

There is no satire in Huxley's presentation of this Neo-Platonic idealism. In fact, the narrator's commentary affirms the progression that has begun as Poole and Loola find in each other emblems of absolute beauty. Contrasting their nuptial night with the orgiastic Belial Night, he comments on the absence of "caterwaulings" and "saxophones pleading for detumescence" and calls for a music blending the best of Mozart, Bach, and Beethoven that "transcends the Romantic integration of the tragic and the joyful, the human and the daemonic." He then wonders:

And when, in the darkness, the lover's voice whispers again of

> A mortal form indued
> With love and life and light and deity,

is there already the beginning of an understanding that beyond *Epipsychidion* there is *Adonais* and beyond *Adonais*, the wordless doctrine of the Pure in Heart?

The question is mainly rhetorical, for Poole is launched on his quest. In the final scene of the book, the lovers come upon William Tallis's grave as they journey across the Mojave Desert to join the "Hots," and Poole supplies from "Adonais" the antidote to Tallis's despairing epitaph taken from the same poem. Tallis's tombstone carries the message of vanished hopes from the fifty-third stanza of Shelley's elegiac poem; Poole reads from the hopeful fifty-fourth stanza, which speaks of a "Light whose smile kindles the Universe" and of a "Benediction which the eclipsing Curse / Of birth can quench not." His progression from repression through animalism to romantic love and on to this affirmation of a mystical absolute augurs a future understanding of the doctrine of the "Pure in Heart."

Huxley does not, however, end with the Shelley quotation but with a curious action calculated to be ambiguous. After reading from "Adonais," Poole cracks an egg on Tallis's headstone and scatters the shell over the grave. Whether this is intended as an oblique allusion to the egg as a symbol of immortality and the action meant as a consecration, or, as Keith M. May maintains in his study of the novel, serves as a desecration,[6] remains unclear. And, in terms of the overall impact of the novel, its positive or negative meaning may be pointless to ponder. For if Huxley's principal purpose in writing *Ape and Essence* was to warn of the dangers of nuclear war and of the mentality that makes it conceivable, he accomplishes his aim within the two-thirds of the book devoted to dealing with the horrific effects of man's self-damnation. The last thirty pages or so, despite their positive message of individual transcendence, do little to dispel the lingering images of a savage society in which the ape is in ascendance.

Both *Brave New World* and *Ape and Essence* reflect Huxley's distrust of the idea of progress, the bedrock of late nineteenth-century and twentieth-century optimism.

The Victorian version of this ideal held that "things" by their very nature were constantly in the process of evolving into something better. Two world wars dimmed such all-encompassing utopianism for the twentieth century, but faith in the progress of science and technology as the means of furthering civilization remained firm. Huxley's two dystopian novels challenge the notion that scientific and technological advancements inevitably bring about improvement and illustrate the point he makes in *Brave New World Revisited* (1958) that the "Nature of Things is such that nobody in this world ever gets anything for nothing." In these novels, future generations pay for the twentieth century's blind faith in technology, and the price exacted for progress is human freedom.

Island

The epigraph Huxley chose for *Brave New World* from Russian religious and social philosopher Nikolay Berdyayev's *The End of Our Time* is an apt expression of Huxley's own skepticism about the utopian ideal. The last sentence of the quotation especially fits his view that the "perfection" of utopia is at the price of freedom. It translates: "And perhaps a new age will begin, an age in which the intellectuals and the cultivated class will dream of how to avoid utopia and to return to a non-utopian society, less perfect and more free."

In *Island*, his final novel, Huxley dreams of such a society—one "non-utopian" in the sense that it avoids sacrificing freedom to perfection and, also, in the sense that it represents an ideal Huxley took to be potentially realizable. He describes the book in one of his letters as a "kind of pragmatic dream" and to reinforce the notion of the practicality of his fantasy begins the novel with a quotation from Aristotle: "In framing an ideal we may assume what we wish, but should avoid impossibilities." Although the imaginary Palanese society pictured here comes close to being an earthly paradise, it differs from mythical versions of such a place in that it is entirely the product of human effort and good will and thus, theoretically, possible to achieve. As one of the characters explains, Pala is neither Eden nor the Land of Cockaigne even though it is a nice place to live; but "it will remain nice only if everybody works and behaves decently."

As a man-made paradise, Pala is a blending of the best of two worlds, of East and West. It is the kind of civilization the Arch-Vicar in *Ape and Essence* envisions with horror when he considers what might have been the alternative if Belial had not triumphed and seen to it that East and West took the worst from each other. If Eastern mysticism had made sure of the proper use of Western science, if the Eastern "art of living" had refined Western energy, and if Western individualism had tempered Eastern totalitarianism, the result would have been, says the Arch-Vicar, "the kingdom of heaven." Happily, as the Arch-Vicar sees it, these possibilities remained unrealized, allowing Belial to establish his hell on earth. Almost twenty-five years after portraying this hell in *Ape and Essence*, Huxley gives shape in *Island* to the vision of heaven adumbrated in his earlier novel.

However, rather than the worldwide "kingdom of heaven" of the Arch-Vicar's nightmare, Huxley's fully developed version of this utopia based on the best from East and West is located on a remote island and is surrounded by all the horrors of modern civilization that precipitated Huxley's warnings in his two anti-utopian fictions. Like the island communities in *Brave New World* to which Alpha individualists are banished and the Northern California colony in *Ape and Essence* to which those who are still human flee for refuge, Pala is a "tiny oasis of humanity" in the midst of a "worldwide wilderness of monkeys." It is the preserve of a creative minority of Eurasian people who have chosen sanity over insanity, self-determination over servitude. Heirs of a culture crafted out of the combined insights of a Scottish doctor and a Palanese king, these inhabitants of the "Forbidden Island" practice the Eastern art of living fully as human beings in a society that has managed to rid itself of the "two thirds of sorrow that's homemade and gratuitous." But the outside world is encroaching, drawn to Pala by the prospect of oil; and the threat of impending destruction hanging over this utopian society constitutes the backdrop against which Huxley focuses on the elements that have turned Pala into a paradise.

The novel opens with an accidental intrusion into Pala. Will Farnaby, British journalist and agent of Western oil magnate Lord Aldehyde, wrecks his boat on the shore of the forbidden island and comes to consciousness, injured and confused, on the rock face above the coast. Except for the insistent voice of a mynah bird calling out "Attention!" (an imperative that serves as a theme in the novel), there is nothing in the opening scene to indicate the locale. Much of the scene shifts into past tense and deals with Farnaby's earlier life in London, revealing his guilt over relationships with his wife Molly and his mistress Babs. In his semiconscious condition, he replays his cavalier rejection of Molly for the more sexually desirable Babs and remembers Molly's death, for which he feels responsible; he recalls giving himself over completely to sensuality with Babs in a room transformed by the red and green neon lights of a Porter's Gin sign. When the room turned green, he was no longer able to escape from thoughts of death, the "Essential Horror," through sex; for "Bab's rosy alcove became a womb of mud and, on the bed, Babs herself was corpse-colored, a cadaver galvanized into posthumous epilepsy."

These fragments of memories make it apparent that
Farnaby, like many of Huxley's characters that have trouble
with sexual relationships, is psychically wounded. In fact,
in many ways, he is a composit of other such characters
from the earlier novels. He has some of Spandrell's Baude-
lairean cynicism and fascination with death, which they
both call the "essential horror"; he shares Gumbril's inability to make commitments and, also like Gumbril, he is
haunted by the loss of the only person he ever loved; like
Chelifer, he once wanted to be a poet and turned out to be
a second-rate journalist; and in much the same way as Walter Bidlake torments himself for betraying the woman who
loves him for the vamp who uses him, Will feels guilty for
rejecting Molly for Babs, who has also tossed him aside for
another lover.

All of these resonances from other characters and other dilemmas make Will Farnaby and his problems seem
slightly dated in a novel that is presumably set in the sixties. As Harold H. Watts points out, Farnaby is "really a
contemporary of Anthony Beavis in *Eyeless in Gaza*
(1936), who was a product of Edwardian culture and its
particular kinds of hypocrisy and bigotry,"[7] despite Huxley's intentions of making him contemporary with the time
in which *Island* was written. Although Will is something
of an anachronism, one of his chief functions in the novel
is as a contrast to the saner, more balanced Palanese. And as
a representative of the "twenty-nine hundred million mental cases" outside Pala and a product of the conditions
that, Huxley believes, make for insanity, Farnaby serves
well Huxley's purpose of showing the superiority of the
Palanese ways of thinking and living to those of other
cultures.

Although Farnaby is allowed to remain at Pala to recov-
er from his physical injuries, the main work of restoration
that takes place during his stay is psychological and spiri-

tual. The work begins with his first encounter with the islanders—ironically two precocious children, Tom Krishna
and Mary Sarojini MacPhail, who already know more
about dealing with traumatic experiences than the English-
man. Mary especially is adept at the sensible Palanese practice of exorcising demons by confronting them, and she
takes over Farnaby's case with such assurance that he appears to be the child and she the adult. Leading him systematically through the events that have brought on his
shock—the shipwreck, the long climb up the cliffs, his
being terrorized by snakes and falling from a precipice—
she makes him face his fear and recognize that he has escaped relatively unscathed. Her treatment is a practical
application of the philosophical principles of "Attention"
and "Here and now" that the mynah bird has been taught
to repeat; for as Farnaby pays attention to the present,
he realizes that the things he is afraid of "happened
yesterday."

While Farnaby's most persistent demons are not so
easily displaced, the program of "Here and now" into
which Mary Sarojini initiates him with this first lesson is
the one through which other, more experienced guides
lead him. However, these lessons come later in the novel
since the program Huxley sets for Farnaby for the bulk of
the book dictates his providing the outsider's perspective
on Pala and functioning as an audience for those commis-
sioned to explain the various Palanese solutions to social
problems. His contacts with several of the natives—Dr.
Robert MacPhail, great-grandson of one of the architects of
Pala's social system; Susila MacPhail, the doctor's daughter-
in-law; Vijaya Bhattacharya, the doctor's assistant; nurse
Rahda Appu and her lover Ranga Karakuran—are all calculated to reveal some facet of Pala's well-considered way of
doing things. Further, Farnaby's change of heart (or, more
precisely, mind) cannot come too quickly because of the

role he has to play as the "serpent in the garden." His fortuitous entrée into Pala has given him the chance to work on behalf of Lord Aldehyde in securing oil concessions for Southeast Asia Petroleum and to earn a handsome bonus; thus there is the dramatic irony that as Farnaby is introduced to a paradise built on the exclusion of capitalism, he at the same time means to be the agent through which Western "progress" comes to Pala.

Part of the tension in the novel stems from the question of whether or not Farnaby will be party to the destruction of the Palanese way of life, although it is a foregone conclusion that Pala cannot remain isolated from the rest of the world for long. Just outside the island, Colonel Dipa, military dictator of Rendang, stands ready to make his move once his young protégé Murugan Mailendra, the Raja of Pala, reaches his majority and becomes the ruler of the country. These two, plus Murugan's mother, the Rani, are even more venomous serpents in this paradise than Farnaby, and each has separate reasons for wanting to exploit the country's oil resources. Colonel Dipa wants to extend his power by becoming the prime minister of an oil-rich United Kingdom of Pala and Rendang; Murugan, promising a policy of "Continuing Revolution," wants to undo the earlier reforms of Pala his mother has taught him to hate and to grab the power and wealth Colonel Dipa has taught him to love. The Rani has slightly more unusual motives. Founder of a mystical religious organization called the Crusade of the Spirit, she proposes to use the wealth gleaned from Pala's resources to further her brand of "Pure Spirituality." Although the Rani speaks in the language of Eastern mysticism similar to that of the other, more genuine Palanese, Farnaby recognizes her kinship with Joe Aldehyde: "A female tycoon who had cornered the market, not in soya beans or copper, but in Pure Spirituality and the Ascended Masters."

While the schemes that will destroy the work of a hundred years are being finalized, Farnaby is being introduced to the various aspects of a society designed to ensure that each individual is "as perfectly free and happy as it's possible to be." The irony of the timing is calculated and telling; for in structuring the novel so that Pala is doomed from the start, Huxley points up the "precariousness of happiness," which one of his letters suggests he saw as a theme. For Huxley, the central issue of *Island* is not so much the preservation of the imaginary utopia as the presentation of the conditions that could plausibly make a community ideal. Thus while Pala's perilous position as a utopia in the midst of a mad world constitutes the framework of the novel and Will Farnaby's eventual "enlightenment" illustrates the potency of the Palanese philosophy, it is Huxley's conspectus of an ideal community that lies at the heart of the novel.

In this outline of a good society that manages to balance stability and individuality, freedom and happiness, Huxley deals with topics that had long intrigued him and had been the subjects of essays in books such as *Ends and Means* (1937), *The Perennial Philosophy* (1945), *Tomorrow and Tomorrow and Tomorrow* (1956), and *Brave New World Revisited* (1958). His ideas on education, population control, eugenics, technology, consumerism, social organization, economics, non-attachment, the family, and drugs are among those that find a place here. But in terms of Farnaby's process of psychic healing, and also, in terms of Huxley's attempt to reach a positive resolution of issues that have been perennially problematic in his fiction, the three most significant subjects with which he deals in *Island* are religion, sex, and death.

Although in both *Ends and Means* and *The Perennial Philosophy* Huxley recognizes a certain correspondence between Christianity and Eastern religions, particularly in their emphasis on contemplation as a way of intuiting God, or the "Divine Ground," his antipathy for much of Christian doctrine is evident in all of his novels. In *Island*, it comes through in the contrast between the deleterious effects of Christianity on Farnaby and the salutary effects of Tantrik Buddhism on the islanders. Farnaby's guilt over having rejected the good (Molly) and chosen evil (an adulterous relationship with Babs), expressed sardonically in his quotation from St. Paul about the "good that I would, I do not, and the evil that I would not, that I do," is attributed to Christianity's failure to offer its followers concrete methods of realizing the ideals inherent in its teachings. His nihilism stems in part from the hypocrisy of his parents, whom he calls "Bully Boozer" and "Christian Martyr" because his father escaped into the bottle and his mother into religion from the horrors of their marriage; it is also a reaction to the pointlessness of his Aunt Mary's death, of World War II, and of all the cumulative suffering in the world for which he finds no answers or cure in Christianity. In his introduction to Dr. MacPhail, Farnaby describes himself as "the man who won't take yes for an answer." Recognizing in his guest the unhappiness behind the bravado, Dr. MacPhail tells Susila that Farnaby is "too clever to believe in God or be convinced of his own mission. . . . His muscles would like to act and his feelings would like to believe; but his nerve endings and his cleverness won't allow it."

Farnaby's cynicism and fragmentation are seen to be the results of Christianity's emphasis on God as transcendent, an idea that Huxley presents as destructive in this novel because it emphasizes the separation of man, God, and nature. The positive contrast to this notion in the Palanese society is the view of the godhead as immanent, present in man and the cosmos. Farnaby first encounters an expression of this philosophy in the old Raja's *Notes on*

What's What, and on What It Might Be Reasonable to Do about What's What. Pointing out that a dualistic belief in God as "Wholly Other" obscures the fact that "all existence is relationship" and leads to conflicts and frustrations, the Raja writes of another way, a non-dualistic "reconciliation of yes and no lived out in total acceptance and the blessed experience of Not-Two." On this level of consciousness, the distinctions between sacred and profane, subject and object, the ego and "other" disappear, revealing the central truth around which the Palanese have built their lives and their society: *"tat tvam asi,* thou art That, mind from Mind is not divided."

Although this view of the totally integral relationship of all things may lead to a religious experience, it is not to be considered tantamount to religious dogma; for the recognition of "thou art That" breaks down the barriers commonly held in dualism to exist between the religious and the secular, as Farnaby learns in a frank discussion of sex with two of his young hosts. Through the avenue of *maithuna,* or the "yoga of love," the Palanese simultaneously practice contemplation and birth control. According to Radha Appu, an enthusiastic proponent of *maithuna,* the awareness brought about by this kind of yoga allows the participants to pay attention at once to the self and the not-self and facilitates the process of regaining the paradise of "sexuality diffused throughout the whole organism" that tends to be lost after childhood. However, more relevant for Farnaby's situation is the fact that in this approach to sex there is no division between sin and sacrament, mind (or spirit) and body. Like most of Huxley's split men, Farnaby has difficulty reconciling his sexuality with the other aspects of his nature and thinks his only choices are between asceticism and hedonism, the mind or the body. When Radha tells him of another alternative—a way of experiencing sex as a harmony of mind and body rather than a separation—he realizes that his lovemaking with Babs was a "kind of deliverance" in its way, but not of the sort Radha describes. Instead of bringing awareness, it was an escape from awareness and from his "odious daytime self."

In making sex a means of gaining mystical awareness in his utopia, Huxley resolves the separation between the sensual and the religious that has been endemic to his novels. Another of the persistent problems he addresses once more and attempts to settle is that of gratuitous or "unwarranted" death. Keith M. May conjectures that a connection exists between Huxley's several episodes dealing with the death of the good or harmless person and the effect on him of the deaths of his mother and his brother;[8] but whatever the reason, Huxley's novels are replete with such episodes: Grace Elver's death from food poisoning; Little Phil's death from meningitis, which so disturbed Maria Huxley; and, especially, the deaths of Theodore Gumbril's and Anthony Beavis's mothers. In *Island*, there are three deaths through which Huxley explores both the problem of the "unwarranted" death and the different ways in which those who are bereaved cope with them. Two are in the background—the deaths of Farnaby's Aunt Mary from cancer and of Susila MacPhail's husband Dugald; in the foreground is the death of Lakshmi MacPhail, the doctor's wife of thirty-seven years.

From an account Huxley wrote of his wife Maria's last days (contained in a footnote in the collected letters), it is apparent that the scene in the novel in which Lakshmi's death is eased by the suggestions her husband gives her to go forward "completely unencumbered" into the Clear Light of the Void bears a close resemblance to events surrounding Maria's death. Huxley wrote in this account: "I continued to remind her of who she really was—a manifestation in time of the eternal, a part of forever unseparated from the whole, of the divine reality; I went on urging her to go forward into the light." In a similar way Lakshmi, who taught the doctor to be human, as Huxley admits Maria taught him, is comforted in her dying. But the significant fact in this fictional death scene is that Lakshmi is awake and at peace even in her pain. Aided by her husband and daughter-in-law to focus attention on the here and now—the love surrounding her, the sound of music and the Courting Dance outside—Lakshmi experiences her death as a freedom from ego and self-pity. This peaceful yoga of death contrasts sharply, as Farnaby notes, with the struggle and finally drugged oblivion of his Aunt Mary.

The mourners' responses are also different in this case not only from Farnaby's reaction to death as the "Essential Horror" but also from that of Huxley's other characters compelled to deal with such apparently gratuitous deaths. While Huxley does not minimize the loss here, he suggests that the problem of human suffering and death takes on a new dimension in the eternal scheme of things when one discovers the implications of the Buddha's message, "I show you sorrow, and I show you the ending of sorrow" Dr. MacPhail and Susila first face the fact of Lakshmi's death by participating in her dying and then are consoled by the recognition of an ending of sorrow. On the other hand, Farnaby, Gumbril, and Beavis are haunted by death because they have tried to escape from the fact of it and have failed to submit to the cycle that brings an end to sorrow. The wisdom Huxley intends to impart in this novel is that acceptance rather than flight or egoistic cynicism is the key to dealing with the pain of both life and death. That view is nicely summed up in an explanation Farnaby is given of "Tantra": "If you're a Tantrik, you don't renounce the world or deny its value; you don't try to escape into a Nirvana apart from life, as the monks of the Southern School do. No, you accept the world, and you make use of it; you make use of everything you do, of everything that happens to you, of all the things you see and hear and taste and touch, as so many means to your liberation from the prison of yourself."

Farnaby is helped most in his progress toward liberation by the ministrations of Susila MacPhail, whose recent widowhood prompts him to expose his confusion and grief over his aunt's and Molly's deaths. With calculated sarcasm, he tells her the whole story of the past that torments him, beginning with his unsatisfactory family relationships and going on through his acute sense of unreality in which people became "phantom maggots," his marriage to Molly as an escape, and his flight to the vulgar sensuality of Babs. Turning to Susila for help and wisdom, he asks her how one learns to forget. Her answer is a repetition of the Tantrik philosophy of acceptance that constitutes the core message of the book: "It isn't a matter of forgetting. What one has to learn is how to remember and yet be free of the past. How to be there with the dead and yet still be here, on the spot, with the living."

In the final chapter of *Island*, while Colonel Dipa and Murugan are making ready for the coup that will put Pala on par with the rest of the world, Farnaby at last confronts his fears and comes to accept the fact of sorrow from which he has been fleeing. Ironically, he faces reality in a trance induced by the *"moksha*-medicine," a drug made from mushrooms that the Palanese call the "reality revealer." To the uninitiated, such as Murugan and the Rani, the *moksha*-medicine is merely dope; but to the other islanders, it is an avenue of liberation from the ego and a path to mystical enlightenment, producing an experience equivalent to that brought about by prayer and fasting. As Vijaya, one of the initiates, explains, the *moksha*-medicine "prepares one for the reception of gratuitous graces—premystical visions or the full-blown mystical experiences."

This is the same language Huxley uses in *The Doors of*

Perception in describing his experience with mescaline and promoting the benefits of a pharmacological way to self-transcendence. In the earlier book, he speaks of his mind-altering experience as a "gratuitous grace" and as a "Door in the Wall" of inner and outer reality. But the positiveness with which he advocates the use of mescaline and the *moksha*-medicine is in direct contrast to the negativeness with which he presents the use of *soma* in *Brave New World*. The difference in his attitudes in *Island* and in *Brave New World* has to do with the use made of the drugs. In the anti-utopia, *soma* provides an escape from everyday reality, introducing a state of happy oblivion that blots out awareness of the here and now. In the pragmatic utopia of *Island*, the *moksha*-medicine offers heightened consciousness and is a means both of seeing everyday reality in a new light and perceiving the eternal truths that lie behind it.

However, as Huxley admits in his account of his own experience, fear as well as understanding can be engendered by a hallucinogen; and fear is one of Farnaby's strong reactions. In *The Doors of Perception*, Huxley maintains that "in theological language, this fear is due to the incompatibility between man's egotism and the divine purity, between man's self-aggravated separateness and the infinity of God." As he translates this idea into his fictional presentation of Farnaby's experience, he depicts Farnaby plunged into the hell of his terrorizing memories of death and suffering, out of which he senses that the "dark little inspissated clot that one called 'I' was capable of suffering to infinity." But with Susila's help, he emerges from hell into a heaven of incandescent light; and as this vision fades, returning him to his "daytime self," Farnaby weeps with gratitude for "being at once this union with the divine unity and yet this finite creature among other finite creatures."

The novel closes with the same reminder with which it

opens: a call to "Attention." As the troops invade the island, Farnaby realizes that he is witnessing the beginning
of sorrow for the Palanese. Yet in the course of his brief
stay in Pala, he has come to understand that contained
within the beginning is the end—that heaven and hell are
"indissolubly wedded."

C. S. Ferns contends that "because it is his last novel,
Huxley's critics vie with one another in investing *Island*
with a spurious finality."[9] Whether one agrees with Ferns
that the novel promises a new direction for developments
that were yet to come or considers *Island*, as Jerome Meckier does, Huxley's "final, Herculean attempt at resolution
and synthesis,"[10] it is obvious that there is a sense of optimism in *Island* unprecedented in Huxley's other fiction.
Perhaps this stems from his having worked through problems that had lingered from one novel to another. Certainly
in structuring the book as a positive response to issues
raised in *Brave New World*—the indivisibility of freedom
and suffering in particular—the moralistic Huxley of the
sixties redresses the vision put forward by the amused cynic of the thirties. Where Huxley's evolving ideas about the
possibilities of the individual's development and potential
for self-transcendence within the context of an increasingly complex world would have led is indeterminable. What
is apparent is that in framing his ideal and setting it forth in
Island, Huxley was not looking to construct the "compen-
satory dream" he thought typical of utopians; rather, he
was attempting to present a plan that would, as he often
says in his essays, "take in all the facts."

4

Improving the Illusion

Conjecturing from the vantage point of 1955 that *Brave New World* might turn out to be Aldous Huxley's most enduring book, Francis Wyndham calls the novel (which has lived up to his prediction) the "last destructive work by an essentially destructive writer."[1] This idea that in the novels after 1932 Huxley moved away from the locus of his talent in shifting from corrosive satire to affirmative didacticism has now become a commonplace of criticism. Although the later fiction is not devoid of satire, just as the earlier novels (*Those Barren Leaves* and *Point Counter Point* in particular) are not free from moralizing, it is obvious that with *Eyeless in Gaza* (1936) the "amused Pyrrhonic aesthete" of the twenties and early thirties has given way to the serious moralist. The result of Huxley's change from iconoclast to proselyte is a body of fiction aesthetically flawed by extensive exposition of ideas but still curiously interesting for the uniqueness of the social and metaphysical schemes it contains.

The problem Huxley poses for himself at the time of the writing of *Eyeless in Gaza* and articulates through Anthony Beavis, the novel's protagonist, is "how to combine belief that the world is to a great extent illusory with belief that it is none the less essential to improve the illusion? How to be simultaneously dispassionate and not indifferent, serene like an old man and active like a young one?" Essentially, the dilemma is how to go about improving the world without ascribing to it ultimate reality and how to be dispassionate without being detached. As in his Lawrentian phase, when he held to the ideals of completeness and life worship, Huxley still regards the world as being "manifestly in regression" and views detachment through idea-mongering as a "death-substitute." Also as before, the problem and the solution both reside within the individual psychology. Society is sick because individuals are maladjusted; cure individuals and regenerate society. However, instead of seeing the Lawrentian mind-body balance as the remedy for the individual's dualism and, coincidentally, for society's ills, Huxley takes up the view that transcendence of the ego is the best means of achieving personal unity and, ultimately, of bridging the separation not only between individuals but also among nations. The way to achieve this self-transcendence and to use the awareness it brings for social good, Huxley suggests, is through non-attachment—a mystical approach that involves "direct insight into the real nature of ultimate reality" and the "practice of disinterested virtues."

Such a change in perspective dictated the necessity for replacing the Complete Man of *Point Counter Point* with a more satisfactory ideal. In *Ends and Means* (1937), Huxley describes this ideal as the "Non-attached Man." Systematizing in his tract some of the ideas advanced initially in *Eyeless in Gaza*, Huxley maintains: "The ideal man is the non-attached man. Non-attached to his bodily sensations and lusts. Non-attached to his craving for power and possessions. Non-attached to the objects of these various desires. Non-attached to his anger and hatred; non-attached to his exclusive loves. Non-attached to wealth, fame, social position. Non-attached even to science, art, speculation, philanthropy. Yes, non-attached even to these. For, like patriotism, in Nurse Cavell's phrase, 'they are not enough.'"

Eyeless in Gaza

Eyeless in Gaza is the novel in which Huxley first works through the idea of non-attachment. To some extent autobiographical, it has been called his "conversion" novel.[2] For in tracing Anthony Beavis's growing recognition that philosophical and emotional detachment is "not enough" and his subsequent process of regeneration, Huxley also chronicles his own movement away from the "philosophy of meaninglessness" and Lawrentian "consummate humanity" into an acceptance of spiritual reality. However, rather than accentuating the theme of spiritual insight, the novel's title plays on the idea of spiritual blindness, which is Beavis's condition throughout most of the book. Taken from Milton's "Samson Agonistes," a poem dramatizing the plight of the Biblical Samson, blind and captive of the Philistines in the prison at Gaza, the contextual passage for Huxley's title speaks of defeat and bondage:

> Promise was that I
> Should *Israel* from *Philistian* yoke deliver;
> Ask for this great Deliverer now, and find him
> Eyeless in *Gaza* at the Mill with slaves,
> Himself in bonds under *Philistian* yoke. (38–42)

Other than its concluding with unwavering affirmation, the chief novelty of *Eyeless in Gaza* among the fiction in the Huxley canon up to 1936 is its structure. Consisting of fifty-four chapters designated by date rather than title, the book covers a time period from November 6, 1902, to February 23, 1935, but in a dislocated chronology. For example, the events of chapter one take place on August 30, 1933; chapter two, an excerpt from Anthony Beavis's diary, is dated April 4, 1934; chapter three, carrying the same date as chapter one, continues the sequence of events introduced there; chapter four, dated November 6, 1902, is actually the chronological beginning of the novel; chapter five takes up on December 8, 1926; chapters six through nine continue in chronological sequence from dates established in earlier chapters; and chapter ten picks up on June 18, 1912, and begins a new narrative thread. This juggling of time presents some difficulties and has led at least one reader to the observation that "a card index should not be necessary for the understanding of a work of art."[3] But for all the surface appearance of disunity in the novel, Huxley achieves through his shuffling of time and resequencing of events a clear unity between structure and theme.

One of the key messages of the book is the axiom Beavis jots down in his diary: "Self-knowledge an essential preliminary to self-change." Connected with this message is the theme of memory and the role it plays as an avenue of self-knowledge and, thus, as an agent of change. In establishing the theme in the opening chapter, Huxley evokes Proust and Wordsworth—the first for his concern with recovering the past and making it permanent through memory; the second for his belief in memory as both a moral agent and a mental power connecting each moment with past and future. Against these proponents of the past he sets Anthony Beavis, who on August 30, 1933, the date the novel opens, finds the past an unwelcome intrusion as it is conjured up by some old snapshots. Pictures of his mother, of Mary Amberley, his former mistress, of himself at Eton, call forth a past that he has tried to disconnect from his present; and in mockery of Wordsworth's "And I could wish my days to be / Bound each to each by natural piety" ("Ode: Intimations of Immortality"), he tells Helen Ledwidge, his present lover and daughter of Mary Amberley, "I would wish my days to be separated each from each by unnatural impiety."

At this point in his life, Beavis's singular goal is free-dom—from emotional entanglements, the burden of the past, and introspection. A sociologist, his study of his fellow human beings has been conducted from the safety of distance; his personal affairs are conducted with equal detachment. Like Philip Quarles, he turns to the "higher Life" of ideas as a refuge from commitment and responsibility. And he finds in intellectual constructs even a rationale for the disunity of his life—for his "temperamental divorce between the passions and the intellect." Writing in chapter 11 of his *Elements of Sociology* of the "world in general as though the world in general were like himself," he contends that personality is "just a succession of more or less incongruous states." Naturally, if this is true, it obviates the necessity for achieving consistency within the self, for forging a coherent personality. Ironically, Beavis's postulates, for which he cites Blake and Lawrence in support, echo Huxley's in his essay on Pascal (*Do What You Will*), where he equates consistency with death worship and inconsistency with life and full humanity. Perhaps like Beavis, Huxley writes in this earlier piece of the world as he wants it to be when he maintains that man is a "series of distinct psychological states, a colony of diverse personalities." In any event, this notion seems for a time to have freed him from what he describes as chasing the "absolute in those remote strange regions beyond the borders of the quotidian consciousness." His Complete Man is not obliged to be consistent—only vitally diverse, giving sway to the various facets of his nature. But the views of 1936 are not those of 1929; and it is evident from his undercutting of Beavis's ideas, which are so like those once his own, that Huxley has veered away from his relativistic doctrine of life worship and is ready to chase the absolute.

While undermining his previous views through Beavis, Huxley also makes it clear that despite Beavis's attraction to the Lawrentian idea of the "total man" he does not exactly fit the prescription. Theoretically, Beavis sees that the advantage of the body is as an empirical fact—"it is indubitably *there*." And although he likes to think of himself as a sensualist, he is as divided as Quarles between mind and body, and no more "human." However, the ironic twist in this novel is that even if Beavis were the "total man" idealized in *Point Counter Point*, he would not match the new mold Huxley has in mind. He would be too much of an egoist, too preoccupied with living according to his own impulses to be of much benefit to anyone else. In *Point Counter Point*, Rampion harangues the world for being sick, predicts its destruction, and goes back to practicing the art of integral living. Pointing out to Quarles that the modern "industrial smell" and decent living are probably irreconcilable, he advises: "In the meantime, at any rate, we must shovel the garbage and bear the smell stoically, and in the intervals try to lead the real human life." But according to the program Huxley has outlined in *Eyeless in Gaza*, social responsibility is a part of living integrally. Beavis's "conversion" through the aegis of anthropologist and pacifist Dr. James Miller entails his recognizing that knowing the good also involves doing the good—that unity within the individual life implies unity of all life and imposes the obligation to "improve the illusion."

Yet the Beavis of August 1933 is some distance from this insight. Not only is he unconcerned with universal unity, he is obstinate in denial of the possibility of any connectedness or pattern in his own life. Chapter 3 shows him trying to deal with memories evoked associatively. He tells Helen she looks "like a Gauguin"; his words trigger thoughts of Paris and seeing his first Gauguin with Mary Amberley when he was twenty. To shut out the importunate past, he kisses Helen's shoulder; the scent of her skin, reminiscent of salt and smoke, transports him back to boyhood and Brian Foxe's description of the smell of flints struck together in a chalk pit as being like "smoke under the sea." The recollection of Brian, the friend whom he betrayed and who has now been dead nearly twenty years, prompts Beavis to consider the function of memory. He wonders if the pictures from the past have any significance and why they come to haunt him when, at age forty-two, he thought he had them safely stored away in the "cellars of his mind." Wishing to believe that the past is without meaning for the present and memory is without pattern, he decides: "Somewhere in the mind a lunatic shuffled a pack of snapshots and dealt them out at random, shuffled once more and dealt them out in different order, again and again, indefinitely. There was no chronology."

The structure of the novel seems at first glance to confirm Beavis's notion about the lack of pattern in either his life or his recollection of it. The Beavis of chapter 1 is unregenerate, fragmented in the new Huxleian sense of refusing to admit any connection between the "selves" of different periods or psychological states. The Beavis of chapter 2, almost eight months later, is ready to recast both his book on the elements of sociology and his life into a new and cohesive shape. These would, in fact, appear to be disparate selves. But as the novel progresses beyond the first two chapters, filling in events and rounding out characters mentioned only briefly in the introductory pages, the link between the regenerate and the unregenerate Beavis emerges. Rather than being structured along the lines implied in Beavis's model, as a series of snapshots dealt out at random, the book comes closer in organization to illustrating Miller's theory of cause and effect. Maintaining that nothing ever happens by chance, Miller tells Beavis when they first meet: "One takes the card the conjuror forces on one—the card which one has oneself made it inevitable that he should force on one. It's a matter of cause and effect." This idea of Miller's fits in with his belief that "means determine ends" and that the means a person chooses predict the results he gets. The several narrative strands of *Eyeless in Gaza* tend to bear out this view of cause and effect and of the crucial element of choice in determining the pattern that forms.

Except for two chapters dated 1931 dealing with events separated by two years from those before and after them, the briefest segment of the novel is that which is chronologically the first in the record of Anthony Beavis's life. Spanning from November 6, 1902, to January 1904, it begins with the death of his mother and concludes with his father's remarriage. Several of the people of importance to Beavis's later life are introduced: Mary Amberley, who is present at Maisie Beavis's funeral and nine years afterwards becomes Beavis's mistress; James Beavis, the uncle who influences his nephew to become an atheist; John Beavis, the protagonist's philologist father, against whose standards his son shapes his life; Mark Staithes, with whom Beavis goes to Mexico, where he meets Miller; Hugh "Goggler" Ledwidge, whom Helen Amberley marries and of whom Beavis makes a cuckold; Brian Foxe, for whose suicide twelve years later Beavis is largely responsible; and Mrs. Foxe, Brian's mother, whose Christian humanism creates the first glimmer of desire in Beavis to do good. The four chapters in this segment reveal that despite the mature Beavis's rejection of the sentiments expressed in Wordsworth's "Intimations Ode," Wordsworth is right in his assertion that "The Child is Father of the Man." Young Beavis's attempt to divorce his emotions and to divert his mind from the reality of his mother's death, to know that she is dead only "superficially, as one knows, for example, that thirty-five comes after thirty-four," foreshadows his future emotional detachment. In a similar fashion, the scene at school in which the boys torment Goggler Ledwidge and then turn on Brian Foxe when he protests their maltreatment of the pathetic boy reverberates into the future. In particular, Beavis's ridicule of Brian to garner the favor of Mark Staithes portends his eventual betrayal of Brian to please Mary Amberley.

In terms of chronology, the next section of the book covers a period from June 18, 1912, to July 24, 1914. It picks up with Beavis and Brian at Oxford and traces two love affairs: the totally sexual relationship of Beavis and Mary and the entirely chaste relationship of Brian and Joan Thursley. The lines between the two sets of couples meet when Beavis, on a dare from Mary, kisses Joan and she construes his detached, momentary sensuality as an expression of love. With the final four of the ten chapters focusing on this phase of Beavis's life, the pace of the novel slows as form corresponds to substance; for the subject of the narrative here up to the final chapter in the sequence is Beavis's procrastination in telling Brian the truth about the episode with Joan. His cowardice prevents him from taking any action; and when finally Brian receives a letter from Joan telling him that she and Anthony are in love and breaking off her romance with him, Beavis refuses to take responsibility. Closing his mind to his own culpability, he perceives himself as a "man of good intentions, maliciously prevented, at the eleventh hour, from putting them into practice." His capacity for self-protective deception continues in the meeting with Mrs. Foxe after Brian's body is found. Rather than tell her of his part in driving Brian to suicide, he allows Mrs. Foxe to berate herself for loving her son too possessively and, thus, to assume full responsibility for his tragic death.

Although the episode dealing with Brian's death is the climax of the 1912–14 narrative, much of this section of the novel revolves around the contrast between Beavis and Brian, particularly in terms of their social and moral val-

ues. At Oxford, both join the Fabians. But while Brian is
intent on finding a way to do something direct to bring
about social improvement, Beavis elects to retreat into his
private world of scholarship. He rejects Brian's idealistic
Christian liberalism, preferring personal freedom to social
responsibility. Ironically, one of his arguments against action is the assertion that mysticism, which he can accept as
a "metaphysical theory," is the way to direct knowledge of
the truth. When Brian accuses him of using skepticism
against religion and mysticism against scientific reasoning,
he maintains: "I don't value single-mindedness. I value
completeness. I think it's one's duty to develop all one's
potentialities—*all* of them." In an earlier Huxley novel like
Point Counter Point, such a paean to completeness would
imply the reconciliation of mind and body. However, within the context of the discussion here, the idea for a new
sort of completeness involving mystical awareness is being
advanced—even though it is evident that at this stage
Beavis is using the idea sophistically in order to justify his
inclination to remain free of any governing philosophy. Yet
the seed is there for his eventual acceptance of Miller's
mystical doctrine.

Beavis's assertion of his freedom and Brian's idealism
carry over from the social to the moral realm. To his detri-
ment, Brian has such an idealized view of love that he
cannot admit to feelings of sexual desire without profound
guilt. Ashamed that he desires Joan "in the wrong way," he
retreats from her, making both of them miserable. Beavis,
on the other hand, enjoys completely the forbidden fruit
of licentiousness with Mary Amberley, nine years his senior and a woman of vast sexual experience. Mary is Mrs.
Viveash (*Antic Hay*) raised to the tenth power—bored,
restless, seeking amusement in sex, both self-destructive
and cruel. And, like Gumbril, who sullies the purity of his
relationship with Emily for the sake of Mrs. Viveash's en-

tertainment, Beavis turns the story of Brian's and Joan's pure love into a comic anecdote for Mary's delectation. Playing the "scientific vivisector," he anatomizes Brian's preoccupation with chastity, forgetting that Brian is his friend. When he tries to retract his cruelty, Mary taunts him with being too innocent and sets in motion the events that will destroy Brian.

The third section of the novel focuses mainly on Mary and her daughter Helen, who share certain characteristics. It begins on December 8, 1926, twelve years after Beavis has broken off his relationship with Mary, and at a point in time when he reenters her social circle. The events in six of the ten chapters clustered between 1926 and 1928 take place on December 8. These six chapters serve the function of reintroducing characters from the past, such as Mark Staithes, Hugh Ledwidge, and Gerry Watchett, one of Beavis's Oxford acquaintances and Mary's current lover. In addition, they introduce a new narrative element that begins with Helen's budding sexuality and traces her experimental flirtation with the ethereal Hugh, her seduction by Gerry and the abortion that follows, and, finally, her capture of Hugh as a husband.

Although, unlike Mary, Helen is in search of love rather than distraction, her marriage and affairs turn out almost as disastrously as her mother's. When the novel opens, beginning the fourth narrative segment, she carries "her hell about with her." The marriage to Hugh is a farce, and the relationship with Anthony is an emotionless vacuum. Wishing to play Dante to Helen's Beatrice, to elevate her idealistically to a "divine presence," Hugh cannot cope with Helen's sensuality or the everyday reality of marriage. Wanting in her only a sexual partner who neither gives nor asks for love, Beavis reduces her to nothing more than a desirable body of pleasing form and texture. Caught between two men that she categorizes as the "spiritual lover"

and the "epicurean sage," Helen lives in a "hell of empti-
ness and drought and discontent."

Both Helen and Anthony use sex as a diversion from
other realities—Helen to escape from the meaningless
present, Anthony to blot out memories of the past. The
turning point in their relationship—and also one of the
three epiphanic moments in the novel that contribute to
Beavis's change—occurs after they have made love on the
sunroof. From an airplane overhead a dog suddenly hurls
into space and crashes onto the roof, splashing the lovers
with blood. The episode is both grotesque and symbolic.
In his study of the novel, Peter Bowering metaphorically
likens the "dog from the skies" to a "thunderbolt of a
wrathful Jehovah" and observes that "it is almost literally
the *deus ex machina*—dog 'interpreted kabbalistically
backwards, signifies God.'"[4] On a less supernatural level,
the incident is the traumatic climax of Helen's almost path-
ological aversion to certain aspects of physical reality, but
only in subsequent scenes dealing with her earlier life does
the pattern leading up to this climax become apparent. The
episode in which she steals a kidney from a butcher's shop
on a dare and is reduced to tears with revulsion serves as a
prelude to her reaction on the roof. More immediately in
the chronology, the kidney becomes associated with Hel-
en's dying kitten: "She was disgusted by the poor little
beast, couldn't bear to touch him as though he were one of
those filthy kidneys." These two symbols converge again
as Helen, half-delirious after an abortion, dreams of holding her sister's baby and, suddenly, the "thing she held in
her arms was the dying kitten, was those kidneys at the
butcher's, was that horrible thing which she had opened
her eyes to see Mme. Bonifay nonchalantly picking up and
carrying away in a tin basin to the kitchen."

The mangled body of the terrier on the roof is the
culminating symbol in this series, evoking all the others

and crystallizing the horrors of the past into one moment. It is this coalescing of past with present that makes credible Helen's complete devastation by an incident that is shocking but not necessarily psychologically immobilizing. However, in terms of plot, Helen's emotional reaction serves as the catalyst for Beavis's response, which is the key element in the scene. When Helen breaks down, Beavis is unexpectedly moved to pity and love and, for the first time, sees her as a person. This recognition, both of Helen as a complex personality with an existence outside the context of sexual pleasure and of his own capacity for emotion, makes Beavis realize that he "had been a fool" to insist on an impersonal relationship. Ironically, when he goes to make a new start with Helen, she has fled, and the two parallel lines fail to meet. But Beavis's journey of self-discovery has begun.

The second epiphanic moment in his journey occurs six days later. Spending a sleepless night listening to the insistent sound of the cicadas and a cock crowing in the distance, Beavis is reminded of D. H. Lawrence's *The Man Who Died*, a novel that celebrates the irrepressible energy of life in the natural world. For Lawrence, that energy on the animal level was enough—in fact, was preferable to the "squalid relationships of human beings advanced halfway to consciousness." But, Beavis decides, Lawrence's view had been limited by his not having seen biological life under a microscope; thus, compared to the energy of, for example, the sperm and the egg in the fertilization process, Lawrence's emblems of animal life seem "only feebly alive." Beavis further concludes that in his insistence on life Lawrence was mistakenly concentrating on *means* rather than *ends*—that life, or energy, should not be the goal but the means to a purpose. Recognizing that he has made a similar mistake in regarding knowledge as an end rather than a means to something else, Beavis has a sudden

intuitive insight into what his existence might be were he
to turn his "raw material of life, thought, knowledge" into
a "finished product."

At this juncture, he is uncertain how or where to begin
and fears appearing foolish; but before he has time to talk
himself out of abandoning the "quiet life" for some more
active pursuit, Mark Staithes comes along to persuade
Beavis to accompany him to Mexico. Staithes, a Commu-
nist who believes that death is the one thing yet undefiled
by modern civilization, proposes to go help start a revolution in Oaxaca, but more for the danger of it than for
Marxist principles. From the standpoint of the anticipated
thrill of risking his life in a coup, the trip turns out to be
futile for Mark, who injures his knee en route to the revolution and misses it. But for Beavis, the Mexico adventure
represents the turning point in his life. It is at this stage that
he meets Dr. Miller, physician, anthropologist, pacifist, and
practitioner of F. M. Alexander's methods of physical coor-
dination and "proper use of the self." Miller appears suddenly like someone divinely sent to diagnose Beavis's
problems and to show him how to make a "finished product" of his life; and this epiphany brings about Beavis's
conversion. When Mark, completely unreceptive to Miller's
optimistic view of man's innate potential for goodness, sardonically suggests that he and Anthony "huddle together
among the cow-pats and watch the doctor trying his best
anthropological bedside manner on General Goering,"
Beavis's response indicates that he has already decided on
another, less cynical course: "I think I shall go and make
myself ridiculous with Miller."

The fifth section of the novel traces Beavis's evolving
self-awareness and social commitment through his journal
entries for 1934 and 1935. Beginning with the recognition
that his "besetting sin" is an indifference to other people,
Beavis sets out to learn how to love. The lesson involves

discovering the difference between detachment and non-attachment. Through his lifelong refusal to be "bothered by people," Beavis is practiced in the art of detachment; but non-attachment is a less egoistic pursuit. It requires moving beyond total self-interest into care and concern for others. Underpinning the concept of non-attachment is the idea of fundamental unity even in diversity—the view that unity constitutes the absolute to be sought within the individual psyche, among individuals and nations, and as the final truth or "divine Ground" of being.

Under Miller's guidance, Beavis first turns his attention to transforming the separate parts of his make-up, described by Miller as "one clever man and two idiots," into a unity. This entails attempting to develop his emotions and his body to the level of his intellect. Working on the principle that "mind and body are one," he undertakes certain physical exercises in conjunction with mental concentration in order to forge the mind-body connection. From self-awareness, he then directs his efforts toward becoming aware of others and developing the emotional capacity for love. It is interesting that as Beavis makes love rather than sensuality his aim, he becomes continent and discovers that in the process of loving the "potentialities for goodness in all human beings," eroticism seems relatively unimportant.

As a way of trying to put love into practice in the realm of politics, Beavis joins an organization of pacifists and begins to work on behalf of a nonviolent solution to international problems. The journal chronicles his growing discipleship in acting on Miller's doctrine that social change is predicated on changes within the individual and that international peace is dependent upon harmonious "inter-individual relations." In the last chapter of the novel, he faces the test of his convictions. Warned by a group antagonistic to his pacifist position that he will be attacked if he gives his scheduled speech, Beavis is tempted to abandon the cause and go back to his old life as spectator and vivisector, looking on from his "private box and making comments." But in meditating on unity as the ultimate good, the beginning and the end, he realizes that division is the condition of life as well as the evil against which he must struggle; thus his choice is against the separation characteristic of his former life. At the conclusion of the novel, the non-attached Beavis emerges, prepared to act on the basis of his ideal of universal unity: "Dispassionately, and with a serene lucidity, he thought of what was in store for him. Whatever it might be, he knew now that all would be well."

In *Eyeless in Gaza*, Huxley overcomes the ambivalence evident in *Those Barren Leaves* concerning the possibilities of a mystical solution to the problem of division. He also redresses what some readers have viewed as a weakness in the remedy proposed in the earlier novel. For example, C. S. Ferns suggests that the "trouble with the solution which Calamy explores is that it is so *private*; to find reality, he believes it necessary to have absolute solitude."[5] While Beavis's answer also involves contemplation, it does not require his removal from the world; in fact, it takes him more into direct contact with people than was true with his old habit of indifference. Unlike Calamy, he realizes that meditation can be a "bolt-hole" from unpleasant reality and quietism can become "mere self-indulgence." Thus in Beavis's solution, meditation is a means to an end that has practical consequences in the social realm of interpersonal relationships. Almost as if in response to his earlier, less satisfactory approach to living in accord with "ultimate reality," Huxley has Beavis recognize and record in his diary that: "To live contemplatively is not to live in some deliciously voluptuous or flattering Poona; it is to live in London, but to live there in a non-cockney style."

After Many a Summer Dies the Swan

Mr. Propter, the contemplative seeker of eternal truth and Miller counterpart in Huxley's next novel, lives in neither India nor London but in California, where Huxley settled in 1938. *After Many a Summer Dies the Swan* (1939) is the first of the fiction published after Huxley's immigration to the United States and, consequently, the first of his novels with an American setting. The new locale provides Huxley with fresh opportunities for satire— particularly of American acquisitiveness and of the West Coast as the brashest example of the country's vulgar materialism. Seen through the eyes of Jeremy Pordage in the novel, like Huxley a recent arrival from England, the panorama of Southern California reveals a bizarre mixture of gaudy commercialism, diluted spirituality, and cultural crassness. Signs announcing "Fine Liquors," "Turkey Sandwiches," "Go to Church and Feel Better All the Week," and "What Is Good for Business Is Good for You" appear in rapid succession as Pordage takes his first tour through Los Angeles. Even more astonishing to this scholar of "curiously rarefied" tastes are the Beverly Pantheon Cemetery, where marble scrolls inscribed with Biblical quotations contrast with statues of nubile females, and the pseudo-Gothic castle of Jo Stoyte, the hard-driving, uneducated magnate whose hatred of culture underlies his urge to possess art treasures in profusion and to dominate educated men like Pordage. Filled with a jumble of priceless objects, all "perfectly irrelevant" to each other, Stoyte's castle seems to Pordage emblematic of the "no-track mind" of an idiot.

Stoyte's "no-track world" of unrelated objects is mere-

ly a microcosm of society's "idiot-universe" of irrelative
values and moral confusion. Huxley's central message in
this novel, for which Mr. Propter as the exemplar of non-
attachment is the spokesman, is that "actual good" exists
only outside time and the individual ego and that "potential good" is anything that liberates one from the bondage
of time, personality, and egoistic craving. With this doctrine, Huxley not only rejects the ideal of full humanity set
forth in *Point Counter Point* but also turns away from the
resolution of social humanism proposed in *Eyeless in Gaza*. As he defines it here, "potential good" is incommen-
surate with the "strictly human level," which equates with
time and craving. It exists only below and above the human level, in the proper functioning of the physiological
organism and in the mystical "knowledge of the world
without desire or aversion." And since he regards any ideal
except that of liberation as a projection of ego, even such
humanitarian causes as peace, which in the preceding novel Beavis embraces and works to promote, serve only to
deflect evil from one channel to another. Beavis's recognition in the final pages of *Eyeless in Gaza* that separation is
evil and yet is the condition of life on the temporal level
brings Huxley to the brink of the conclusion with which
he begins *After Many a Summer*—the view that the evil
inherent within time must be overcome through transcending time and gaining an "immediate experience of
eternity."

Only Mr. Propter, who lives outside the Stoyte estate
and whose non-attachment to self and things serves as a
"standing reproach" to Jo Stoyte, his childhood classmate,
achieves this mystical ideal. For although he is the positive
philosophical focus of the novel, his example and message
of liberation are principally the backdrop for Huxley's satire of a host of characters illustrating the evils of time and
craving. Reverting to the house-party formula of the earlier

books, he brings together within the Stoyte castle a collection of egoistic "oddities" attached in varying ways to the temporal world. Most are familiar types in the Huxley menagerie: there is Jeremy Pordage, the mother-dominated aesthete and sexually infantile "Peter Pan"; Dr. Sigmund Obispo, Stoyte's personal physician and the novel's representative cynic; Peter Boone, the doctor's research assistant and a naive idealist; Virginia Maunciple, Stoyte's young mistress, worshipper at both the shrines of Eros and Our Lady; and Stoyte, an aging tycoon with a horror of death, whose obsession with physical longevity contrasts with Mr. Propter's interest in "psychological eternity." Like the fabled character in Tennyson's "Tithonus," the poem from which the novel's title is taken, Stoyte wants immortality; and such is his desperate fear of death that, unlike the original, who finds immortality without everlasting youth more cruel than death, this modern Tithonus can conceive of no condition in life that would be worse than death.

Stoyte's quest for prolonged life is key to the novel's theme, which revolves around the difference between eternity and immortality, and also to its plot. Haunted by the prospect of dying and of facing the damnation foretold in the Biblical warning, "It is a terrible thing to fall into the hands of the living God," Stoyte supports Dr. Obispo's research into the mysteries of the carp's longevity in the hope that science will save him from death and divine judgment. While Obispo plays on Stoyte's paranoia, keeping the "old sack of guts," as he views his benefactor, dependent upon him with sex hormones and a show of solicitude, he also seduces his "concubine-child." Virginia becomes enslaved to the violent eroticism of the sadistic Obispo, who, like Spandrell in *Point Counter Point*, uses sex as a means of perversion and domination. To throw Stoyte's suspicions off the track, she pretends interest in

Pete Boone, whose Quixotic idealism blinds him to his Dulcinea's decadence. These activities within the human zoo are analogous to the behavior of the baboons kept on the estate as research animals. The scene in which a formidable old baboon relaxes his guard over his submissive female and a younger male seizes the opportunity to mate with her sets up the situation for which the human triangle of Stoyte, Miss Maunciple, and Obispo is the parody. Miss Maunciple is delighted to find the baboons so human ("Aren't they *human!*"); the irony in the novel, as in *Ape and Essence*, is that the humans are so apish.

This notion of the short distance on the evolutionary scale between man and ape takes on a new dimension in part 3 of the novel. Part 1, consisting of thirteen chapters and the most extensive section of the book, is replete with exposition of Propter's philosophy, against which the unsatisfactory lives of those caught within time are measured. In terms of plot, it lays the groundwork for Obispo's scientifically-engineered conquest, culminating in his seduction of Virginia. Part 2 ties in Jeremy Pordage's work with the Hauberk papers, which he has been employed by Stoyte to catalog, with the theme of rejuvenation and immortality and prepares the way for the fantastic events in the final segment of the novel. Here Jeremy discovers in the eighteenth-century autobiography of the Fifth Earl of Hauberk confirmation of Obispo's theory that within the longevity of the carp lies the secret to human immortality. Excerpts from the Fifth Earl's account of how his youth and sexual vigor are being restored on a diet of raw "fish-guts" constitute a secondary narrative to the main plot line of Stoyte's growing suspicion, which reaches a crescendo with his shooting of Pete Boone, whom he mistakes for Obispo. With part 3, in which Obispo goes to England in search of information about the Fifth Earl and finds him alive, a creature more than two hundred years old that has reverted to a "foetal ape," Huxley introduces briefly the idea of regression from the human to the simian state that turns into the controlling concept on which *Ape and Essence* is predicated.

As Jerome Meckier indicates, the story of the Fifth Earl's rejuvenation in his diary clues the reader to the fact that he is still alive, and, therefore, the "novel's epiphanic last scene is a foregone conclusion."[6] An even earlier hint comes in Mr. Propter's discussion with Pete about the possible effects of prolonging life through scientific means. In conjecturing that such longevity might entail "growing back" instead of "growing up," he not only foreshadows the final scene but also goes on to suggest the "nightmarish" quality of such an existence within time. To the frightened Jo Stoyte, however, to whom death rather than time is the enemy, even the Fifth Earl's brutish existence is not sufficiently nightmarish to quench his desire for immortality. Watching the "foetal anthropoid" that was the Earl hitting the simian creature that more than a century earlier was his mistress, Stoyte considers the advantages of continued life even in light of the disadvantage of becoming an ape: "How long do you figure it would take before a person went like that? . . . I mean, it wouldn't happen at once . . . there'd be a long time while a person . . . well, you know; while he wouldn't change any. And once you get over the first shock—well, they look like they were having a pretty good time. I mean in their own way, of course."

After Many a Summer Dies the Swan is a hybrid novel made up of a mixture of didacticism, fantasy, and satire. Perhaps in anticipation of the criticism the book would likely draw, Huxley attacks in it "so-called good literature," by which he seems to mean both realistic fiction and tragedies. Decrying the lack of theory in "merely descriptive" novels and the lying consolation of the catharsis in tragedy, he regards satire as the only potentially profitable literary form—but, even with satire, "the trouble was that so few good satires existed, because so few satirists were prepared to carry their criticism of human values far enough." Measured by this criterion of far-reaching criticism, which debunks an extensive array of conventional values in the name of some high ideal, *After Many a Summer* would qualify as a "good satire." Here, against the ideal of liberation from self and time, Huxley satirizes practically everything on the temporal level as conflicting with both the eternal reality and the definition of man as "a nothingness surrounded by God, indigent and capable of God, filled with God, if he so desires."

Time Must Have a Stop

During the more than twenty years between the publication of *After Many a Summer Dies the Swan* and of *Island*, the plan for which was conceived as early as 1940, Huxley wrote only three works of fiction, and two of these are slight novellas. *Ape and Essence* (1948), the dystopian fable, extends the idea of human retrogression in time first suggested in *After Many a Summer*; and although the book has what Sybille Bedford calls a "high degree of unbearableness,"[7] it also has some significance as a part of Huxley's utopian trilogy. The other novella, *The Genius and the Goddess* (1955), is more subdued in tone than Huxley's anti-utopian satire on the "death, by suicide, of twentieth-century science" but is also more tedious. It is both a first-person reminiscence of the aging narrator's emergence, thirty years earlier, from "half-baked imbecility into something more nearly resembling the human form" and an exposition on the non-attachment view of dying as "an art"—an idea represented more fully and dramatically in *Island*. Although Huxley rewrote the book several times in an effort to achieve an "easiness" of style, the final version suffers from the monotony of the narrator's uninterrupted monologue and the lack of dramatic action. As George Woodcock observes, "none of Huxley's works reveals quite so boldly the paucity of his powers of visualization."[8]

In *Time Must Have a Stop* (1944), the fully developed novel that immediately succeeds *After Many a Summer*, Huxley returns primarily to the realistic mode of *Eyeless in Gaza* and to the conversion motif. However, in this work he described as a "piece of the *Comédie Humaine* that modulates into a version of the *Divina Commedia*," he takes both a gentler approach to his unregenerate souls and has a firmer grasp of the way to salvation than in his earlier, more structurally complex novel. As a transition book in which Huxley reviews aspects of his own intellectual history and attempts to clarify for himself the nature of his newly arrived at philosophy of non-attachment, *Eyeless in Gaza* seems at times to be as much a voyage of discovery for its author as for its protagonist. In *Time Must Have a Stop*, Huxley knows where he is going, and the controlling idea of the novel is not only disseminated as a certainty but also guides the direction of the narrative.

The central message is presented as a commentary on Hotspur's speech in Shakespeare's *Henry IV, Part I*:

> But thought's the slave of life, and life's time's fool,
> And time, that takes survey of all the world,
> Must have a stop. (V. iii. 81–83)

In the commentary, Huxley contrasts time (associated with selfhood and separation) and eternity (associated with self-transcendence and union):

But Hotspur's summary has a final clause: time must have a stop. And not only *must*, as an ethical imperative and an eschatological hope, but also *does* have a stop, in the indicative tense, as a matter of brute experience. It is only by taking the fact of eternity into account that we can deliver thought from its slavery to life. And it is only by deliberately paying our attention and our primary allegiance to eternity that we can prevent time from turning our lives into a pointless or diabolic foolery.

It is toward this didactic point, which Huxley reserves for the epilogue, that the narrative unswervingly advances.

Set in 1929, the story begins in London with the introduction of Sebastian Barnack, the seventeen-year-old hero of this Bildungsroman, whose development under the influence of a series of tutors constitutes the subject of the main narrative. A shy, self-conscious poet who, like Denis Stone in *Crome Yellow*, tends to think in images, Sebastian sees himself as a possible successor to Keats and Wordsworth—although more capable of rendering the modern realities than either of the romantics. For example, in the "as yet unnamed and unwritten poem" of his imagination, which he mentally composes for most of the novel, he would temper Keatsian idealism with a "spice of the absurd" and present the Wordsworthian sense of "something infused" in conjunction with "the horror" infusing it in order to speak with a contemporary voice.

At this stage of his life, Sebastian is what he later calls a "spiritual embryo, undeveloped, undelivered, unillumined" and remains so for several years; but there are early auguries of the mystery to which he will eventually be drawn, although at the time Sebastian is unaware of their spiritual significance. One temporal analogue of the transforming power of the eternal "Intelligible Light," which equates to God or the "divine Ground," is evident in the scene in which the gaslights at night transform the horrid architecture of The Primitive Methodist Chapel into what Sebastian regards as an "unfathomable pregnant mystery." Since he is spiritually blind, Sebastian sees this change only with the poetic eye; but the language in which he renders the transfiguration from everyday ugliness to mysterious beauty has spiritual connotations: "Little squalor! transfigured into Ely, / Into Bourges, into the beauty of holiness." Wondering which is real, the daytime monstrosity that receives the pastor and his flock on Sundays or the illuminated spectacle of "bright little details and distinctions fading upwards into undifferentiated mystery," he finally concludes that the best he can do by way of answer is to reformulate the question in terms of poetry.

Thus for the unregenerate Sebastian, aesthetics serves as the substitute for enlightenment and is the initial attachment binding him to the temporal and the secular. He also has the makings of a sensualist, but in the opening sections of the novel, which focus on his life in London as a period of relative innocence, his eroticism, like his dream of poetic greatness, is an adolescent fantasy. Playing the part of a character out of a William Congreve drama, he regales his cousin Susan with the intimate details of an imaginary affair with Mrs. Esdaile, whom he has fabricated from a picture in a book of Victorian steel engravings, a name found in a telephone book, and a vivid imagination. As with Denis Stone's attempts to seem sophisticated, Sebastian's pretensions of worldliness are comic and accentuate his immaturity. But here the incongruity between the image the young man wishes to project and the reality is heightened even more by the fact that Sebastian is not only inexperienced but also has the look of a "Della Robbia angel of thirteen."

Sebastian's initiation into the real world begins when he leaves London and goes to visit his uncle, Eustace Barnack, in Italy. In this Florentine setting, he encounters three of the people who, in various ways, shape his development. The first of these is his epicurean uncle, who, unlike Sebastian's ascetical father, is a connoisseur of sensual pleasures. Although from the standpoint of the moralistic message of the novel Eustace is spiritually dead, entombed within a sarcophagus of hedonism, he is not an unsympathetic figure either to Huxley or young Sebastian, who finds him an especially appealing contrast to his puritanical father. Eustace's generosity and tolerance, his artistic sophistication, and his witty irreverence for every inhibition to pleasure—from social codes to religion—are magnets for the adolescent; so, too, is the fact that he takes seriously the would-be poet's literary aspirations. And, ironically, it is this apologist for pleasure who points out to Sebastian within the context of a discussion of art that he is likely to be disappointed with real life because creative people "aren't really commensurable with the world they live in." This turns out to be the case with Sebastian, but for reasons other than those envisioned by Eustace. To Eustace, who believes that life is a "fine art," poetry is "beautiful *ersatz*," but, nevertheless, a substitute with which the poet can be content as long as he does not try to venture out into the real world—to "descend into evening clothes and Ciro's and chorus girls." More than a decade later, after Sebastian has fulfilled Eustace's unwitting prophecy, he realizes that both the sensual life and poetry are ersatz realities—that the "habit of sensuality and pure aestheticism is a process of God-proofing."

While Eustace's influence on Sebastian is significant, their interaction is brief. On the first evening of his nephew's visit and less than halfway through the novel, Eustace Barnack, prodigious eater and drinker and the closest character here to the Rabelaisian man of other Huxley books, dies of a heart attack. However, his consciousness continues to infuse much of the remainder of the novel as Huxley, in an unusual technical experiment, attempts to depict Eustace's life-after-death experiences in light of the teachings of *The Tibetan Book of the Dead*. In these segments dealing with posthumous existence, Huxley represents Eustace as a "clot of untransparent absence" confronted by an intense light that illuminates his separateness and invites him into unity with it. This "Clear Light of the Void," searching and beckoning, offers the way to salvation in the eternal dimension; but the disembodied consciousness that is Eustace realizes that participation in the light requires self-abandonment—a total annihilation within the light of his separate identity. Unwilling to give up his sense of self, he struggles to hold on to fragments of memories of his earthly life, protecting himself from the invasion of light and defending his right to remain separate. On occasion, as his mother-in-law and others hold séances to contact the dead, he momentarily experiences bodily sensations, although the body he inhabits is that of the medium. But these sensations of "physiological reality" are sufficient to renew Eustace in his determination to avoid the spiritual truth of knowing himself as he is known, even though it means enduring a self-inflicted hell of alienation.

Eustace's sudden death disrupts Sebastian's hopes of benefiting from his uncle's generosity; but once launched into the Italian scene, there is no turning back from the experiences that will have a lasting impact on his life. Sebastian is "fate's predestined target," as Bruno Rontini, the mystical messenger of the novel, calls him; and the events of his life seem to have a certain inevitability. One such event occurs when he meets Mrs. Thwale and, in his innocence, sees in her the incarnation of his imaginary Mrs. Esdaile. As he shifts his erotic fantasies from the phantom lover to the flesh-and-blood woman, he pictures himself as a "consenting Adonis" and Mrs. Thwale as a voluptuous Venus initiating him into the "incandescent copulation" of the gods. Mrs. Thwale, another of the major influences on Sebastian's life, does, in fact, initiate him sexually; but the seduction has none of the "lascivious innocence of heaven" pictured in his idealistic dreams. Veronica Thwale is a Circean temptress in the tradition of Myra Viveash (*Antic Hay*) and Mary Amberley (*Eyeless in Gaza*)—a woman who enthralls men and keeps them the slave of their passions—and her seduction of Sebastian is an "almost surgical research of the essential shamelessness." To the romantic young Sebastian, introduced to a maniacal frenzy of lovemaking quite in contrast to his fantasy of "ethereal intoxication," the experience is best described as that of "twin cannibals in bedlam."

Mrs. Thwale turns out to be one of the people from the Italian sojourn who has a part in Sebastian's later life, as does Bruno Rontini; but since she is, as George Woodcock observes, the "one character completely negative and therefore completely damned"[9] in the novel, while Bruno is the only completely enlightened character, their roles are calculatedly different. Veronica cultivates the sensual side of Sebastian, enticing him, years after their first sexual encounter, to betray his wife; Bruno makes his appeal to the spiritual possibilities in Sebastian, attempting to awaken him to the "fact of eternity." It is Bruno who, in his initial meeting with Sebastian in Florence, draws the analogy between him and the saint whose name he shares yet realizes that, in this young man, seraphic beauty masks spiritual blindness. Calling Sebastian "fate's predestined target," Bruno foresees that suffering and the martyrdom of the self will be required for Sebastian to achieve the "beatific vision" of which he is deprived.

Although Bruno eventually becomes the agent of Sebastian's enlightenment, ironically it is he who is the target of a chain of events set in motion by the adolescent's folly. For within the context of the narrative dealing with Sebastian's development is a tightly constructed plot that traces the "genealogy of an offence," the culmination of which is

Bruno's arrest. The antecedent of the offense is Sebastian's obsessive desire for a suit of evening clothes, a necessary accoutrement for a dinner party to which he has been invited and, more important to him, an outward sign of his maturity. To his father, a political activist with socialist sympathies, the suit would be a class symbol, and he refuses to provide his son with this hallmark of upper-class distinction. Eustace promises to outfit his nephew in Italy but dies before he can carry out his plan. More grieved over his dismal prospects of ever having the dinner attire than the death of his uncle, Sebastian decides to act decisively on his own behalf by selling a Degas drawing Eustace had given him the evening before and buying the clothes himself. After he sells the drawing to the dealer Weyl at a fraction of its value and places his order with the tailor, the legal heir of Eustace's estate, Daisy Ockham, brings her accountant to catalog the contents of the palace and discovers that the Degas is missing. Unable to prove his ownership and afraid to confess his actions, Sebastian appeals to Bruno for help in retrieving the drawing from the charlatan Weyl.

As Bruno listens to Sebastian's plight, he advises his drawing up a "family tree of the offence," pointing out that such a mechanism "makes one realize that nothing one does is unimportant and nothing wholly private." The truth of this observation is borne out in succeeding events. Naively, Sebastian imagines that once he has returned the drawing, the "children of his lie would either remain unborn or else be smothered in their cradles, and the lie itself would be as though it had never been uttered." But his actions have consequences for other people: a servant girl is blamed for the theft of the Degas; the servants retaliate by killing the toy Pomeranian that is the constant companion of old Mrs. Gamble, Eustace's mother-in-law; and Weyl, angry at Bruno's forcing him to give back the drawing, has Bruno arrested by the Fascists. The 1929 chronicle closes with Sebastian's realization of the pain caused by his seemingly harmless machinations but also concerned that the problem of the dinner clothes remains unsolved.

The epilogue, dated January 1, 1944, focuses on a regenerate Sebastian, whose conversion is recounted as a memory. Taking stock of the past on this New Year's Day, Sebastian remembers the suffering for which he has been responsible—the death of his wife during a miscarriage after learning of his affair with Veronica, Bruno's illness after his imprisonment—and his attempt to expiate the guilt by taking care of Bruno before his death from cancer. Although this section deals with the birth process of the "spiritual embryo" under the skillful midwifery of Rontini, it omits the epiphanic moment. Unlike Miller and Propter, the saints of *Eyeless in Gaza* and *After Many a Summer*, Bruno persuades more by example than words, and the evidence of his "joyful serenity" in illness and death convinces Sebastian of the efficacy of the mystical way.

Although edification is one of Huxley's chief aims in *Time Must Have a Stop*, as it is in all of his later fiction, here he wisely reserves the majority of the philosophical exposition for the book's final section. In so doing, he remedies the problem of interrupting the narrative with didactic digressions that especially mars *After Many a Summer*. The *Comédie Humaine* leading up to the 1944 segment dramatizes convincingly the pointless and diabolic "foolery" of lives bound up in attachments to the world of time and craving. The epilogue, wherein Sebastian lays down his "Minimum Working Hypothesis" for those who reject organized religion and humanism but are not "content to remain in the darkness of spiritual ignorance," presents Huxley's mystical solution. A prelude to *The Perennial Philosophy*, which was published the year after *Time Must Have a Stop*, this "Minimum Working Hypothesis" asserts:

> That there is a Godhead or Ground, which is the unmanifested principle of all manifestation.
>
> That the Ground is transcendent and immanent.
>
> That it is possible for human beings to love, know and, from virtually, to become actually identified with the Ground.
>
> That to achieve this unitive knowledge, to realize this supreme identity, is the final end and purpose of human existence.
>
> That there is a Law or Dharma, which must be obeyed, a Tao or Way, which must be followed, if men are to achieve their final end.

In the period following *Time Must Have a Stop*, which many readers would agree with Keith May is "Huxley's best performance in fiction in the last twenty-seven years of his career,"[10] Huxley continued to believe in, and to work from, these basic tenets of mysticism. The utopian society depicted in *Island* is a fictional representation of the way in which Huxley thought they might be put to practical use; for despite his de-emphasis in both *After Many a Summer* and *Time Must Have a Stop* on social reform as he accentuates the "higher utilitarianism" of seeking "unitive knowledge of the divine Ground," which he saw as man's final end, Huxley continued to devote his work to the interim process of "improving the illusion."

5

Huxley as *Pontifex:* Bridge Builder

In *Time Must Have a Stop*, Huxley gently satirizes a young intellectual named Paul De Vries in his quest for "bridge-ideas" that might link the "island universes of discourse"—span the "gulfs separating art, science, religion and ethics." In some ways, Huxley is probably satirizing his own penchant for trying to find connections between the disparate fields of knowledge; for throughout his career as a prolific writer of both fiction and nonfiction, his theme and his approach was that of integration—the integrated life and the integration of knowledge from universes often regarded as incommensurable. Turning again to the idea of bridge building in the series of lectures delivered in 1959 at the University of California, Santa Barbara, he suggests that the role of *pontifex*, or bridge builder, is an appropriate one for the literary person concerned with "the human situation": "The function of the literary man in the present context, then, is precisely to build bridges between art and science, between objectively observed facts and immediate experience, between morals and scientific appraisals."

He also admits in these lectures that "there is a great problem facing the man of letters who tries to build bridges." What he has in mind is the difficulty the artist faces in making of the facts and theories of science the emotionally engaging material for art; but there is also the problem, as Huxley's fiction reveals, of rendering these materials dramatically within an art form. More concerned with ideas than fictional technique, more by inclination a moralist than a fictionist, Huxley wrote first to inform and only secondarily to entertain. And if, as Anthony Burgess says, his fiction sometimes "nags at human stupidity when it should be getting on with the story—well, we accept the didacticism as an outflowing of the author's concern with the state of the modern world."[1] From the standpoint of drawing from the many universes of discourse to address the contemporary problems, no artist has proven to be a more adept *pontifex* than Aldous Huxley.

Notes

1. The Life Theoretic

1. See Aldous Huxley's introduction to *The Letters of D. H. Lawrence* (New York: Viking Press, 1932), x.
2. Grover Smith, ed., *Letters of Aldous Huxley* (London: Chatto & Windus, 1969). All quotations from Huxley's letters are from this edition.
3. Francis Wyndham, "The Teacher Emerges," "A Critical Symposium on Aldous Huxley," *London Magazine* 2, no. 8 (1955): 51–64.
4. Alexander Henderson, *Aldous Huxley* (New York: Russell & Russell, 1964), 13.
5. Grover Smith in *Letters of Aldous Huxley*, 39, says the exact date of the onset of the infection that caused Huxley's near blindness is unknown; Sybille Bedford, *Aldous Huxley* (New York: Alfred A. Knopf/Harper & Row, 1974), 32, sets it in the winter of 1911.
6. Julian Huxley, ed., *Aldous Huxley, 1894–1963, A Memorial Volume* (New York: Harper & Row, 1965), 60. This book will hereafter be referred to as *Mem. Vol.*
7. Ibid., 60.
8. Ibid., 34.
9. Bedford, *Aldous Huxley*, 70.
10. Ibid., 130.
11. *Mem. Vol.*, 18.
12. Harry T. Moore, ed., *The Collected Letters of D. H. Lawrence* (New York: Viking Press, 1962), vol. 2, 1123.
13. Ibid., 1096.
14. M. C. Dawson, *New York Herald Tribune*, February 7,

1932, 5; I.M.P., *New York Herald Tribune*, March 6, 1932, 15.

15. *Mem. Vol.*, 19.

16. Grover Smith in the *Letters* indicates that Huxley's script was never used. Ronald W. Clark in *The Huxleys* (London: William Heinemann, 1968) maintains it is possible that some of his material was used, although no one at MGM seems to know for certain.

17. *Mem. Vol.*, 158.

18. Huxley was fond of quoting William Blake, visionary poet of the nineteenth century.

19. In her biography of Huxley, Bedford first suggests that he took mescaline, LSD, or related substances a total of nine to eleven times in ten and a half years. Later in the book, she sets the total number of drug experiences at twelve based on evidence from Laura Huxley.

20. *The Tibetan Book of the Dead* is a text used in Tibetan Buddhism to guide the dying through the intermediate state between death and rebirth.

21. Bedford, *Aldous Huxley*, 628.

2. The "Incomplete Man" in the Fiction of the Twenties

1. Edwin Muir, "Aldous Huxley: The Ultra-Modern Satirist," *Nation*, 122 (February 10, 1926): 144–45.

2. J. W. Krutch, *New York Herald Tribune*, October 14, 1928, 1.

3. C. S. Ferns, *Aldous Huxley: Novelist* (London: Athlone Press, 1980), 26.

4. T. S. Eliot, "The Love Song of J. Alfred Prufock," *The Complete Poems and Plays* (New York: Harcourt, Brace & World, 1952).

5. Norman Friedman, "Forms of the Plot," *The Theory of the Novel*, ed. Philip Stevick, (New York: Free Press, 1967), 145–66.

6. Ferns, *Aldous Huxley*, 65.

7. J. W. Krutch, *Literary Review* of the *New York Evening Post*, December 29, 1923, 403.

8. Evelyn Waugh, "Youth at the Helm and Pleasure at the Prow," "A Critical Symposium on Aldous Huxley," *London Magazine* 2, no. 8 (1955): 51–53.

9. Joseph Bentley, "The Later Novels of Huxley," *Aldous Huxley: A Collection of Critical Essays*, ed. Robert E. Kuehn (Englewood Cliffs, NJ: Prentice Hall, 1974), 142–55.

10. Harold H. Watts, *Aldous Huxley* (New York: Twayne Publishers, 1969), 52.

11. Alexander Henderson, *Aldous Huxley* (New York: Russell & Russell, 1964), 114.

12. Robert S. Baker, *The Dark Historic Page: Social Satire and Historicism in the Novels of Aldous Huxley, 1921–1939* (Madison, Wisconsin: University of Wisconsin Press, 1982), 13.

13. Ibid.

14. Harry T. Moore, *The Intelligent Heart: The Story of D. H. Lawrence* (New York: Grove Press, 1962), 216.

15. Jerome Meckier, *Aldous Huxley: Satire and Structure* (London: Chatto & Windus, 1969), 120.

16. George Woodcock, *Dawn and the Darkest Hour: A Study of Aldous Huxley* (London: Faber and Faber, 1972), 151.

17. Moore, *The Collected Letters of D. H. Lawrence*, vol. 2, 1096.

18. Bedford, *Aldous Huxley*, 200.

19. Moore, 1096.

3. Heaven and Hell: The Utopian Theme in Three Novels

1. Frank E. Manuel and Fritzie P. Manuel, *Utopian Thought in the Western World* (Cambridge, Mass: Belknap Press of Harvard University Press, 1979), 6.

2. Bedford, *Aldous Huxley*, 623.

3. Chad Walsh, *From Utopia to Nightmare* (New York: Harper & Row, 1962), 112.
4. George Kateb, *Utopia and Its Enemies* (New York: Free Press of Glencoe, 1963), 126.
5. Peter Edgerly Firchow, *The End of Utopia: A Study of Aldous Huxley's Brave New World* (Lewisburg: Bucknell University Press, 1984), 89.
6. Keith M. May, *Aldous Huxley* (New York: Harper & Row, 1972), 190.
7. Watts, *Aldous Huxley*, 139.
8. May, *Aldous Huxley*, 215.
9. Ferns, *Aldous Huxley*, 213.
10. Meckier, *Aldous Huxley*, 208.

4. Improving the Illusion

1. Francis Wyndham, "The Teacher Emerges," "A Critical Symposium on Aldous Huxley," *London Magazine* 2, no. 8 (1955): 51–64.
2. Peter Bowering, *Aldous Huxley: A Study of the Major Novels* (London: Athlone Press, 1968), 114.
3. Phyllis Bentley, quoted without reference in Ronald W. Clark's *The Huxleys*, 238.
4. Bowering, *Aldous Huxley*, 130.
5. C. S. Ferns, *Aldous Huxley*, 84.
6. Jerome Meckier, *Aldous Huxley*, 161.
7. Sybille Bedford, *Aldous Huxley*, 477.
8. George Woodcock, *Dawn and the Darkest Hour: A Study of Aldous Huxley*, 278.
9. Ibid., 234.
10. Keith May, *Aldous Huxley*, 176.

5. Huxley as *Pontifex:* Bridge Builder

1. Anthony Burgess, *99 Novels: The Best in English Since 1939* (New York: Summit Books, 1984), 24.

Selected Bibliography

I. Books by Aldous Huxley

The Burning Wheel. Oxford: Blackwell, 1916.

Jonah. Oxford: Holywell Press, 1917.

The Defeat of Youth and Other Poems. Oxford: Blackwell, 1918.

Leda. London: Chatto & Windus, 1920; New York: Doran, 1920.

Limbo. London: Chatto & Windus, 1920; New York: Doran, 1920.

Crome Yellow. London: Chatto & Windus, 1921; New York: Doran, 1922.

Mortal Coils. London: Chatto & Windus, 1922; New York: Doran, 1922.

Antic Hay. London: Chatto & Windus, 1923; New York: Doran, 1923.

On the Margin: Notes and Essays. London: Chatto & Windus, 1923; New York: Doran, 1923.

Little Mexican and Other Stories. London: Chatto & Windus, 1924; New York: Doran, 1924.

Those Barren Leaves. London: Chatto & Windus, 1925; New York: Doran, 1925.

Along the Road: Notes and Essays of a Tourist. London: Chatto & Windus, 1925; New York: Doran, 1925.

Two or Three Graces, and Other Stories. London: Chatto & Windus, 1926; New York: Doran, 1926.

Jesting Pilate. London: Chatto & Windus, 1926; New York: Doran, 1926.

Essays New and Old. London: Chatto & Windus, 1926; New York: Doran, 1926.

Proper Studies. London: Chatto & Windus, 1927; Garden City: Doubleday, Doran, 1928.

Point Counter Point. London: Chatto & Windus, 1928; New York: Doubleday, Doran, 1928.

Arabia Infelix and Other Poems. London: Chatto & Windus, 1929; New York: Fountain Press, 1929.

Do What You Will. London: Chatto & Windus, 1929; Garden City: Doubleday, Doran, 1929.

Brief Candles. London: Chatto & Windus, 1930; Garden City: Doubleday, Doran, 1930.

Vulgarity in Literature: Digressions from a Theme. London: Chatto & Windus, 1930.

Music at Night, and Other Essays. London: Chatto & Windus, 1931; Garden City: Doubleday, Doran, 1931.

The Cicadas, and Other Poems. London: Chatto & Windus, 1931; Garden City: Doubleday, Doran, 1931.

The World of Light: A Comedy in Three Acts. London: Chatto & Windus, 1931; Garden City: Doubleday, Doran, 1931.

Brave New World. London: Chatto & Windus, 1932; Garden City: Doubleday, Doran, 1932.

Rotunda: A Selection from the Works of Aldous Huxley. London: Chatto & Windus, 1932.

Texts and Pretexts: An Anthology with Commentaries. London: Chatto & Windus, 1932; New York: Harper, 1933.

T. H. Huxley as a Man of Letters. London: Macmillan, 1932.

The Letters of D. H. Lawrence, edited and with an introduction by Aldous Huxley. London: Heinemann, 1932; New York: Viking, 1932.

Retrospect: An Omnibus of Aldous Huxley's Books. Garden City: Doubleday, Doran, 1933.

Beyond the Mexique Bay. London: Chatto & Windus, 1934; New York: Harper, 1934.

Eyeless in Gaza. London: Chatto & Windus, 1936; New York: Harper, 1936.

The Olive Tree and Other Essays. London: Chatto & Windus, 1936; New York: Harper, 1937.

What Are You Going to Do About It? The Case for Constructive Pacifism. London: Chatto & Windus, 1936; New York: Harper, 1937.

An Encyclopedia of Pacifism, edited by Aldous Huxley. London: Chatto & Windus, 1937; New York: Harper, 1937.

Ends and Means: An Enquiry into the Nature of Ideals and into The Methods Employed for their Realization. London: Chatto & Windus, 1937; New York: Harper, 1937.

After Many a Summer Dies the Swan. London: Chatto & Windus, 1939; New York: Harper, 1939.

Grey Eminence: A Study in Religion and Politics. London: Chatto & Windus, 1941; New York: Harper, 1941.

The Art of Seeing. London: Chatto & Windus, 1943; New York: Harper, 1942.

Time Must Have a Stop. London: Chatto & Windus, 1945; New York: Harper, 1944.

Twice Seven: Fourteen Selected Stories. London: Reprint Society, 1944.

The Perennial Philosophy. London: Chatto & Windus, 1946; New York: Harper, 1945.

Verses and a Comedy. London: Chatto & Windus, 1946.

Science, Liberty and Peace. New York: Harper, 1946; New York: Fellowship Publications, 1946; London: Chatto & Windus, 1947.

The World of Aldous Huxley: An Omnibus of his Fiction and Non-Fiction over Three Decades, edited and with an introduction by Charles J. Rolo. New York: Harper, 1947.

The Gioconda Smile: A Play. London: Chatto & Windus, 1948; New York: Harper, 1948. (Under the title of *Mortal Coils*.)

Ape and Essence. London: Chatto & Windus, 1949; New York: Harper, 1948.

Themes and Variations. London: Chatto & Windus, 1950; New York: Harper, 1950.

The Devils of Loudun. London: Chatto & Windus, 1952; New York: Harper, 1952.

The Doors of Perception. London: Chatto & Windus, 1954; New York: Harper, 1954.

The Genius and the Goddess. London: Chatto & Windus, 1955; New York: Harper, 1955.

Heaven and Hell. London: Chatto & Windus, 1956; New York: Harper, 1956.

Adonis and the Alphabet, and Other Essays. London: Chatto & Windus, 1956.

Tomorrow and Tomorrow and Tomorrow, and Other Essays. (American title of *Adonis and the Alphabet*.) New York: Harper, 1956.

Collected Short Stories. London: Chatto & Windus, 1957; New York: Harper, 1957.

Brave New World Revisited. London: Chatto & Windus, 1958; New York: Harper, 1958.

Collected Essays. New York: Harper, 1959.

On Art and Artists, edited by Morris Philipson. New York: Meridian Books, 1960.

Island. London: Chatto & Windus, 1962; New York: Harper, 1962.

Literature and Science. London: Chatto & Windus, 1963; New York: Harper, 1963.

Letters of Aldous Huxley, edited by Grover Smith. London: Chatto & Windus, 1969; New York: Harper, 1969.

II. Books about Aldous Huxley

Atkins, John A. *Aldous Huxley: A Literary Study*. New York: Roy Publishers, 1956.

Baker, Robert S. *The Dark Historic Page: Social Satire and Historicism in the Novels of Aldous Huxley, 1921–1939*. Madison: University of Wisconsin Press, 1982.

Bedford, Sybille. *Aldous Huxley: A Biography*. New York: Alfred A. Knopf/Harper & Row, 1974.

Birnbaum, Milton. *Aldous Huxley's Quest for Values*. Knoxville: University of Tennessee Press, 1971.

Bowering, Peter. *Aldous Huxley: A Study of the Major Novels*. London: Athlone Press, 1968.

Clark, Ronald W. *The Huxleys*. New York: McGraw-Hill Book Company, 1968.

Ferns, Christopher S. *Aldous Huxley: Novelist*. London: The Athlone Press, 1980.

Firchow, Peter. *Aldous Huxley: Satirist and Novelist*. Minneapolis: University of Minnesota Press, 1972.

_____. *The End of Utopia: A Study of Aldous Huxley's Brave New World*. Lewisburg: Bucknell University Press, 1984.

Gandhi, Kishor. *Aldous Huxley: The Search for Perennial Religion*. New Delhi: Arnold-Heinemann, 1980.

Greenblatt, Stephen J. *Three Modern Satirists: Waugh, Orwell, and Huxley*. New Haven: Yale University Press, 1965.

Henderson, Alexander. *Aldous Huxley*. New York: Russell & Russell, 1964.

Huxley, Julian, ed. *Aldous Huxley, 1894–1963: A Memorial Volume*. London: Chatto & Windus, 1965.

Huxley, Laura Archera. *This Timeless Moment: A Personal View of Aldous Huxley*. New York: Farrar, Straus & Giroux, 1968.

Kuehn, Robert E., ed. *Aldous Huxley: A Collection of Critical Essays*. Englewood Cliffs, NJ: Prentice-Hall, 1974.

May, Keith M. *Aldous Huxley*. New York: Harper & Row, 1972.

Meckier, Jerome. *Aldous Huxley: Satire and Structure*. London: Chatto & Windus, 1969.

Thody, Philip. *Huxley: A Biographical Introduction*. New York: Charles Scribner's Sons, 1973.

Watts, Harold H. *Aldous Huxley*. New York: Twayne Publishers, 1969.

Woodcock, George. *Dawn and the Darkest Hour: A Study of Aldous Huxley*. London: Faber and Faber, 1972.

INDEX

PACE UNIVERSITY LIBRARY

New York, NY 10038

TO THE BORROWER:

The use of this book is governed by rules
established in the broad interest of the university
community. It is your responsibility to know these
rules. Please inquire at the circulation desk.

NOV.   1989